AF527963

DISABILITY AND SOCIAL EXCLUSION IN RURAL INDIA

DISABILITY AND SOCIAL EXCLUSION IN RURAL INDIA

INSA KLASING

RAWAT PUBLICATIONS
Jaipur • New Delhi • Bangalore • Guwahati • Kolkata

ISBN 81-316-0051-3
© Author, 2007

Reprinted, 2015

No part of this book may be reproduced or transmitted in any form or by any means, electronic or mechanical, including photocopying, recording or by any information storage and retrieval system, without permission in writing from the publishers.

Published by
Prem Rawat for **Rawat Publications**
Satyam Apts., Sector 3, Jawahar Nagar, Jaipur 302 004 (India)
Phone: 0141 265 1748 / 7006 Fax: 0141 265 1748
E-mail: info@rawatbooks.com
Website: www.rawatbooks.com

New Delhi Office
4858/24, Ansari Road, Daryaganj, New Delhi 110 002
Phone: 011-23263290

Also at Bangalore, Guwahati and *Kolkata*

Typeset by Rawat Computers, Jaipur
Printed at Nice Printing Press, New Delhi

To my parents

CONTENTS

FOREWORD

HARSH MANDER

Former Director, ActionAid India

Happy be they who understand my strange step when walking and my heavy hands. Happy be they who know that my ears have to be strengthened to understand what is said. Happy be they who understand that though my eyes shine my mind is slow. Happy be they who see yet don't notice the food that drops and falls off the side of my plate. Happy be they who with a smile on their lips encourage me to try again. Happy be they who never remind me that today I asked the same question twice. Happy be they who understand that it is difficult for me to clothe my thoughts with words. Happy be they who listen to me, since I too have something to say. Happy be they who know what is in my heart, though I couldn't express it. Happy be they who see me and love me as I am, as I alone am, and not as some would want me to be.

— Argentinean National Association
for the Promotion of Disabled People

For disabled people, the world is beyond reach. The most ordinary of aspirations: to enter school, work in the fields, go out to worship, get married, the prosaic ingredients of even the most humble person's workday life cycle, is frequently denied to them, even as a distant dream. Despite the most profound and consistent denial of even their minimal human rights, it is remarkable that an estimated 50 million persons with disabilities have remained at the outer periphery of both public policy and social action in India.

More than any other large dispossessed social group, people with disabilities are invisible: in political agendas, in human rights struggles, in development strategies, in social science research. But even more strikingly, rarely do we encounter disabled people in schools, farms, factories, playgrounds, cinemas, streets, markets, temples, mosques, churches or in family celebrations.

We know almost nothing about the existential experience of persons, and even less about women and girls, who live with disabilities in the countryside. What is life really like for them, how do they cope, what do they suffer, what are their dreams?

It is to seek answers to questions like this that a team of researchers fanned out to a sample of villages across two states of India, viz., Rajasthan to the west and Andhra Pradesh in the south, in 2001 and 2003 respectively. The majority of researchers were people with disabilities themselves. The studies were supported by the state government, which approached ActionAid India, to lead a participatory study into rural disability. The researchers, youthful and sensitive because of their own lived experience of disability, were equipped with the basic tools of social science research methodology, and then went out in teams for the study. They camped for at least 4 to 5 days in each village. I accompanied a small leg of their search. Their findings are a harrowing indictment of state and society, and a mirror of a victimised people, who live routinely at the edge, invisible and dispensable to the rest of the world that they inhabit.

Almost invariably, in any village when they would start out by asking how many people with disabilities live in the village, people would reply: "There are hardly 3 to 4 disabled persons in the village". But then a quest would begin for the hidden, forgotten people. Disabled people themselves and their carers would lead the team members to new disabled persons, and they in turn would identify more like them. With wonder, village residents would discover that in their own village, which they thought they knew so well, there may be tens of disabled peoples whose existence they were never aware of. In a village of a 1,000 people, one may discover as many as 50 people with disabilities who lived hidden behind the mud walls of their homes.

One striking finding of the studies was the nearly insurmountable physical and social barriers that the people with disabilities confront in accessing public spaces and common properties. Gaps and failures in village infrastructure like roads, drinking water sources and school buildings disproportionately constrain people with disabilities. Temples are built on hilltops, and degraded forests require people with disabilities to walk longer than is physically feasible for them. More grave are social attitudes of shame and ridicule, beginning often within the family, which further immobilise people with disabilities. The result is a sense of isolation, dependency and pervasive low self-esteem, which the researchers encountered widely amongst people with disabilities.

In particular, people with disabilities felt humiliated by their sense of dependency for sometimes even the simplest acts of daily living, like bathing, eating, and attending nature's call. On many occasions researchers found that in impoverished homes, where all carers had to go out for wage work, severely disabled people were forced to remain without food and care for the entire working day. It is important to recognise that dependence can be reduced significantly by education and medical assistance, but the study highlighted how both were beyond the reach of most rural people with disabilities.

The research found a profound denial of schooling to children with disabilities. In Andhra Pradesh 62 per cent of disabled respondents had never been to school, while the Rajasthan survey found that 53 per cent of disabled people were illiterate.

The studies further found that not a single teacher was trained in working with children with disabilities, nor had special teaching aids. Children with locomotor impairment were able to keep pace in class if they were able to overcome the physical and social barriers to their entry into the class in the first place. However, children who were mentally slow, or speech and hearing impaired, or blind, felt isolated and marginalised in the course of teaching.

No school had ramps or special toilet facilities for its disabled students, making education a daily struggle, especially for physically disabled girls. In Andhra Pradesh, only 1.1 per cent of the students accessed government scholarships for children with disability. Disabled children reported that even water taps were often too high for them to reach.

But the picture was not universally dismal. We visited a high school in village Moinabad (Ranga Reddy district of

Andhra Pradesh), in which a girl with callipers unselfconsciously and cheerfully danced with two classmates in the customary welcome dance for visitors. Likewise, in village Badguna (Nizamabad district), we visited a mother who proudly showed us the achievements of her hearing impaired son, who was ahead in studies of his entire class. As we sat in his home and he solved complex maths problems, two non-disabled friends of his arrived to call him out to play. They communicated effortlessly with sign language, and as we walked around the village later, it was clear that his handicap was no impediment in his acceptance as the leader of the gang of boys.

Both surveys indicated that for disabled children of impoverished rural parents – agricultural workers and small farmers – the chances of going to school, and remaining within it, are especially low. This is particularly the case where mothers have to do wage work to sustain the family, and therefore cannot take the child to school. Girls are more burdened than boys, because they have to look after the household work and take care of their younger siblings. Disability was consistently found to be no barrier only to the conventional domestic duties of housework of girls and women.

Aids and appliances as well as correctional surgery can do a lot to assist a person with disability to overcome the constraints imposed by her biological condition. But although modern technology can potentially greatly enhance both the mobility and communication of people with disabilities, the surveys reveal that even low-cost assistance is beyond the reach of most rural people with disabilities.

The researchers could not find medical records of even a single person with disabilities who underwent corrective surgery or modern medical interventions to reverse or improve their condition. One ANM or woman health worker whom they interviewed said she was aware of only one person with disability in the entire village.

The surveys found that in Andhra Pradesh, 51 per cent of those who had disability and were of working age had absolutely no opportunity to work and were fully dependent on the members of their family. In Rajasthan, the figure was 62 per cent. These included persons with leprosy, visual impairment, and severe mental and multiple handicaps. Although many of these persons, especially blind adults, are capable of doing some productive work, their families and the larger community regarded them to be incapable.

However, with very few exceptions, they had uncertain low-end work, barely averaging 7 to 10 days a month, with niggardly wages. But they reported that even this low-wage employment was available only when other workers were not available, or in peak agricultural periods. Even such employment was highest for persons with physical disabilities, whereas other disabled people like those with hearing impairment were considered unsuitable because of difficulties in communicating work demands. Women are further burdened at work, because in spite of their disabilities, in most cases they are still expected to fulfil all their responsibilities of domestic work, and in addition to earn a living in a highly unequal market.

Low and uncertain incomes mean that many people with disabilities and members of their family routinely live with hunger. Even the coping mechanism of seasonal distress migration is usually barred to such people. In the surveys we encountered very few people with disabilities who received any kind of disability pension, or food aid, to protect them through seasons of hunger. The situation is even more tenuous for old persons with disabilities who lack younger caregivers.

The surveys found the highest, frequently tragic, levels of vulnerability and social exclusion among rural women with disabilities. Most were forced to marry in highly unequal situations, as second wives to older men, widowers or divorced men. The large majority of women surveyed reported that they were treated mainly as unpaid domestic labour and sexual objects, and suffered high levels of physical and psychological domestic abuse, sometimes even desertion. Girls with disabilities, particularly those who are mentally challenged, were found to suffer from routine sexual abuse and unwanted pregnancies.

I recall a poignant visit to the home of a woman called Aliveulu with speech and hearing impairment. She sat in the corner of her mother's home in her village, isolated from all communication in her silent lonely world, her face a picture of settled grief. A member of our team, who was herself hearing impaired, communicated with her in sign language. Soon an animated conversation was in progress. She had been given in second marriage to a man much older to her. Except for sex and hard domestic work, he had no interest in her. She finally left him, and returned to her mother's home, where she felt just a little more valued.

The studies also highlighted the problems of the caregivers of rural people with disabilities. I particularly recall the young mother of two children with congenital multiple disabilities in village Tipparti. One son was three, the other two years older, but both could not move, eat or perform their bodily functions without help. They neither spoke, nor responded, nor even turned on the bed without assistance.

The mother wept that she had not been able to leave her home once in five years because of the unrelenting need to take care of the children. Her husband was an agricultural worker, often drunk, who alone could work outside the home to bring in money and food. Both parents were desperate and spoke of suicide. I have rarely met anyone so decisively exiled from hope as that young mother.

Rural families with members who are disabled were found to carry a variety of burdens: social, economic, psychological. There was a pervasive sense of shame and stigma, and families often felt isolated. A family that went to a temple to ritually offer the hair of a disabled boy Durgareddy in village Vaguvalasa (Vizianagaram district in Andhra Pradesh), was turned away. Many caregivers spoke of their sense of deep despair, and suicide was not infrequently mentioned as a serious option.

In village Shilarmiyagudem (Nalgonda district of Andhra Pradesh), a mentally challenged young woman was being cared for by her elderly grandmother. The girl's parents had committed suicide because they found the burden of the disabled child too hard to bear amidst their poverty. Their old mother was far more resilient, and has fought many years to keep both bodies alive. The villagers said they survived on occasional charity, and there were insinuations of casual sex work. We had neither the means nor the heart to verify their claims.

In this way, across our countryside, shrouded from our collective view and conscience, people with disability and their caregivers somehow are living out their lives, surviving, but only just, most often at the precipice of dark despair. It is probably only when they organise into a social and political collective of voice and assertion, that an uncaring state and society will finally be forced to act.

ACKNOWLEDGEMENTS

This book arose out of a one-year fellowship with ActionAid India. I am indebted to many of its staff members, in particular to its former director Harsh Mander for his insight, encouragement and guidance throughout the writing process. Part of this book is based on surveys carried out by ActionAid in Andhra Pradesh and Rajasthan, and I am thankful to Sandeep Chachra, who initiated the survey, as well as the Hyderabad and Jaipur offices, Raman Mehta and the many researchers involved in its execution. Thanks are also due to Dr Anuradha Naidu and Nithila Baskaran from SABLA for reading a draft of the manuscript and to Professor Anita Ghai for reviewing the social exclusion chapter. I am grateful to Dr Mathew Varghese, President of St Stephen's Hospital, for an insightful perspective on disability prevention and to Javed Abidi, Director of NCPED, for an excellent introduction to employment of disabled people. Most importantly, I remain forever thankful to the thousands of disabled villagers who spoke out and shared their life experiences in the surveys.

LIST OF ABBREVIATIONS

AMLICO	Artificial Limbs Company
ANM	Auxiliary Nurse Midwife
CBR	Community Based Rehabilitation
CII	Confederation of Indian Industries
DPED	District Primary Education Programme
ICDS	Integrated Child Development Scheme
IEDC	Integrated Education of Disabled Children
ILO	International Labour Organisation
ITI	Industrial Training Institute
NCPEDP	National Centre for the Promotion of Disabled People
NHFDC	National Handicapped Finance Development Corporation
NHFS	National Family Health Service
NIMHANS	National Institute for Mental Health and Neurosciences
NSSO	National Sample Survey of India

PHC	Primary Health Centre
POA	Programme of Action
PRA	Participatory Rural Appraisal
PWD Act	Persons with Disability Act
RCI	Rehabilitation Council of India
SEVAI	Society for Education, Village and Improvement
SHG	Self Help Group
UNDP	United Nations Development Programme
VHAI	Voluntary Health Association of India
VRC	Vocational Rehabilitation Centre
WHO	World Health Organisation

1

INTRODUCTION

The Invisible Magnitude

The dusty road of Epuru village in Nellore district of Andhra Pradesh is Subayya's home. Leprosy has left his hands so severely deformed that they can hardly grasp the food for which he begs. He says it has been too long to remember when he last had a proper meal, wore a different set of clothes or travelled by bus. As a child, it would have been impossible for him to imagine that this is what life had in store for him. He grew up under the affectionate care of a loving mother and fondly remembers how he used to escape the village to catch up with the latest Telugu movies with his group of friends. He had been married for four years when one morning he woke up with white patches all over his body. Subayya did not recognise these as early symptoms of leprosy and there were no medical facilities in his or the surrounding villages. In the absence of diagnosis and treatment, his legs and fingers slowly became deformed. When he was later told that the hospital at Venkatgiri provided leprosy medicine he was unable to afford the bus fare to get there. Upon realising that leprosy would take its course unhindered, Subbaya's wife walked out of the house and married another villager with whom she had become involved. This was not to be leprosy's last claim on Subbaya. As his sores grew, he was no longer able to till his land and so passed it on to his brother's son, who subsequently refused to share the profit. With the land gone and his body unfit for agricultural wage labour he found employment as a guard for some fields. Even though it took him more than two hours to get to the fields with his deformed legs, he could at least secure three meals a day and had a regular income. All of this came to an end when his eyesight slowly faded, making it impossible to continue his work as a watchman. With no family, no land and no job, there was no other option but to make the dusty village road his home and rely on the goodwill of the villagers not to let him starve.

Magnitude of Disability

The sheer magnitude of disability in India is enormous. India is home to the largest population of disabled people in the world (Karna 2000), possibly second to China. There is a whole continuum of different estimates of the number of disabled Indians, of which even the smallest is staggering. At the bottom of the continuum, National Sample Survey of India (NSSO) estimates suggest that there were 12 million disabled people in 1981, 16.15 million in 1991 and 18.49 million in 2002, which constitute 1.8, 1.9 and 1.9 per cent of the total population respectively. This is more than the entire population of Denmark, Norway and Finland taken together. But even this staggering figure is a gross underestimate, given that major types of disability such as leprosy and cerebral palsy were not included in the survey.[1] At the top of the continuum of estimates, Baquer and Sharma (1997) allege that as many as 90 million people are disabled in present-day India.

The most widely accepted estimate of the incidence of disability lies between either of these extremes at 4 to 5 per cent of the total population, i.e., 40 to 50 million disabled people in India. This seems plausible for three reasons. Firstly, the UNDP estimates a global average of 5 per cent (Helander 1993). Secondly, the Indian Ministry of Social Justice and Empowerment estimated in 2001 that the disabled population in India is 4.1 per cent of the total population, which amounts to 41 million (cited in Planning Commission 2001). Thirdly, 4 to 5 per cent is in line with levels of disability in other South Asian countries. The official estimates of Nepal, Pakistan and Sri Lanka are 5, 4.9 and 3.9 per cent respectively (UN 1996).

However, the number of Indians whose lives are affected by disability is likely to be much higher. "For every disabled person, it is estimated that at least four members of the immediate family will be directly affected through having to adopt to and meet the needs of their relative" (Krishna et al. 2001: 11). This would amount to 160 to 200 million people – a group larger than the population of Brazil.

Whichever estimate one goes by, the majority of disabled people in India live in rural areas. A rural-urban ratio of 80:20 was born out by both the 1981 and 1991 NSSO surveys (Pandey and Advani 1995), while the 2003 NSSO survey showed a rural-urban ratio of 76:24.[2]

An Invisible Issue

Despite their significant numbers and the enormity of suffering as reflected in Subayya's case study, disabled people in India are invisible to the rest of the world they inhabit. They live outside our collective view and conscience and are conspicuous only by their absence in everyday life, policy and politics, development interventions and research.

We do not tend to see many disabled people in schools, temples, workplaces, markets, weddings and buses or, for that matter, in our homes. Much less so do we encounter disabled people at the various levels of *political decision-making*. "People with disability form one of the most politically invisible and under-represented groups in the country" (Disability DK 2003). Unlike other minority and caste groups, disabled people have not yet established themselves as a special interest group in state or national politics. As a result, their concerns are entirely absent from the political agenda and no politician ever vies for the "disabled vote" before elections.

Nor are their concerns taken into account in *policy making* – instead of disability being included by each ministry in their mainstream policies, the issue is overseen solely by the Ministry of Social Justice and Empowerment. This has resulted in all other ministries viewing disability as a mere welfare issue entirely outside their realm of responsibility.

The same is true for *development interventions*. Practically none of the rural development projects funded by donors or the government take active steps to include the disabled (Seeley 2001). NGOs fare little better in this respect. "Almost none of the mainstream NGOs had even considered including disabled people in their development work until the late

1990s" and still do not have an inclusive approach to working with disabled people. Many of them consider disability a specialist issue that they are not qualified to address (Yeo 2001: 20 f.).

Disabled people's concerns are also excluded from the extra-governmental dimension of politics, i.e. from the mainstream *social movements*. Ghai (2002), for example, notes that the concerns of disabled women have been systematically ignored by the feminist movement. While the disability movement has been gathering momentum since the early 1990s over the drafting and passing of the Persons with Disabilities Act[3], it has yet to become a comprehensive mass movement, encompassing regional and rural groups, that decisionmakers seriously have to reckon with. In the meantime, "much of development ... continues as though they [the disabled] do not exist" (Seeley 2001: 4).

Given the exclusion and invisibility of disabled people from everyday life, politics, policy and development interventions, it is perhaps not surprising that they are absent from *research agendas* as well. "Gathering reliable data on disability has never been considered a high priority among those in positions of power" (Yeo and Moore 2003: 577). The discipline 'Disability Studies' has "so far failed to engage the attention of academicians" in India (Karna 2001: 241) and "as an academic endeavour is still to be recognised as a legitimate field of study" (Ghai 2003: 25). Despite the now widely accepted fact that disability is both a cause and a consequence of poverty, development research too has by and large ignored the issue. Neither the UNDP's Human Development Report nor the World Bank's World Development Report include disability in their indices of development. In India too, the

"National Profile on Women, Health and Development", published by VHAI and WHO (Gopalan and Shiva 2000), does not even mention the word 'disability' on 348 pages. This institutional disinterest in research on disability and development is matched by that of academics: in a search of 44 international development journals, article titles, abstracts and keywords, Yeo and Moore (2003) find that as many as 33 journals had no mention whatsoever of disability or related words over five years.

As a result of this invisibility of disability in everyday life, in policy, politics, development interventions and research we know little about the lives of people who live with disabilities, the majority of whom reside in rural areas. Because disabled people in rural India are a silent and invisible group in spite of their significant numbers, we do not know what life is like for them or what their dreams and nightmares are.

Purpose of This Book

This is where this book comes in. It seeks to shed light on the issues and problems that disabled people in Indian villages face in all spheres of life, be it in school, at work, in village society or when they seek medical care. It is intended to generate an understanding of the barriers that prevent people like Subayya from realising such basic aspirations as sustaining a marriage or working in the fields, so that these barriers may be removed through changes in state policy and civil society action.

The book does so by drawing on two extensive surveys documenting the voices of disabled people in rural India. The two disability surveys in question are unique in their focus, participatory process as well as breadth and depth of issues covered. Their scale is unprecedented in the research of disability in rural India. The first survey was commissioned by the Government of Andhra Pradesh with funding from the World Bank and carried out during March to May 2001 by ActionAid India. The second survey was funded and administered by ActionAid in Rajasthan from June to August 2003, in close consultation with the Rajasthan State Disability Department. The book thus records the experiences of disabled people in the rural areas of one state in the south and one state in the north of the country, the former of which ranks third highest in the incidence of disability in India, while the latter reflects the phenomenon of disability in a state with an average incidence of disability.[4] Seven case studies from other states collected originally as part of ActionAid India's "Listening to People in Poverty Project" are added to the chapters and demonstrate that the problems faced by disabled people in rural India as recorded in the surveys are not state-specific, but are similar across states and can be encountered anywhere in rural India. The book addresses what is a reality for the majority of the disabled in India, i.e. those who live in rural areas.

> It is twelve of clock on a sunny summer day in Silchar in South Assam. Someet slowly crawls down from his bed and peeks out of the room to see if anyone is in the courtyard. Someet's mother has not yet come back from the market. His sisters and the neighbour's children will only come home from school in another three hours. There is nothing to do except wait. Someet feels lonely and bored.

Contd. on next page...

It is not that he never tried. He begged his father many times to send him to school. After all Someet wants to lead a normal life and be like the other children. He wants to go to school and have as many friends as his sisters. But "father says I can escort you to school, but who will bring you back?" The forty to fifty rupees a day his father earns as a rickshaw puller are hardly enough to cover the household expenses, so foregoing income just to accompany his son back home is simply not an option.

But while Someet has resigned himself to the fact that the formal school is beyond his reach, he has found another way to learn. Every evening a private tutor comes into his neighbourhood to teach a group of children for a fee. Someet reaches the meeting place by a mixture of crawling and leaning on walls, with pencil and paper clutched tightly in his hand. The tutor is kind to him – she teaches him along with the other children, but never charges him fees. Someet likes the teacher very much. "I never miss a class", he says.

Someet's father feels dejected because he failed to get his son cured and has lost all hope. "Despite trying I did not manage to help my son", he says. When he first realised that his little son could not raise his hands like other children he took him to see a doctor, who simply said that Someet would not be normal. Someet's father did not know what to do next and so went to the nearest office of the Social Welfare Department to enquire about the possibilities of treatment. He was told that this was the business of another department, but was not even given the address thereof. Not being able to afford private medical care, this was the end of the attempt to cure Someet.

Conception of Disability

"Disability" is a relative term in so far as different cultures define their norms of being and doing differently. Conceptions of disability are therefore highly contextual and subjective. In South Asia, even social deviancy or female infertility are considered by some as serious social impairments (Harriss-White 1996). Similarly, in agrarian economies still largely based on manual labour, conditions such as asthma and tuberculosis, which are usually classified as sickness rather than disability, are experienced as disabling (ibid.). While fully recognising the importance of such social disabilities, conditions of sickness and other forms of impairment, the scope of the term "disability" used in this book is nevertheless restricted to the types of disability conventionally recognised as such, like locomotor disability, visual impairment, speech and hearing impairment, mental retardation, mental illness and leprosy. However, the understanding and conception of these adopted in this book is by no means conventional, but is in line with recent paradigm shifts as will be discussed below.

Traditionally, disability has been viewed exclusively as a medical phenomenon. According to the *medical model*, disability is a biological condition or health problem of individuals. The International Classification of Functioning, Health and Disability (WHO 1980) defines disability as any restriction or lack of ability to perform an activity in the manner or within the range considered normal for a human being. This is the definition of disability adopted by the Government of India (Alur 2003). In the medical model, which has also been described as a "deficit model" (Lang 2002), disability is predominantly conceived as a deviation from the normal and essentially as a problem. The solution is thought to lie in medical treatment, the objective of which is to "make" the disabled person as "normal" as possible. In this view people with permanent impairments are failures of the system. Disabled people in the medical model are considered passive and helpless recipients of medical care and have no active role to play in planning and implementing the programmatic interventions intended for them.

The medical model of disability has informed much of government policy as well as NGO interventions. It implies a charity approach, regarding disabled people as needy and requiring welfare measures. This attitude is reflected in the fact that many state governments label disability in negative terms, such as 'Nishakt', the official term for disability in Madhya Pradesh, which depicts a person who does not have the requisite strength to carry forward his or her activities. The title "Restoring the Disabled to Usefulness in Tamil Nadu" of an article published by Indian social work academics in 1997 shows how deeply this view is entrenched even in academic circles (published in Kohli 1997).

The evidence presented in this book proves the medical model wrong. The experiences of disabled people in rural India which the book records suggest that this model does not adequately capture the phenomenon of disability. What prevents disabled people in villages in Rajasthan and Andhra Pradesh from living a life like anyone else, going to school, participating in family celebrations and working in the fields is not the individual's impairment, but how society interprets and reacts to it. Life is made difficult not so much by the individual's medical condition, but mainly by a hostile physical and social environment which excludes disabled people from all spheres of village life. The chapter on education shows that disabled children drop out of school not because their legs do not carry them there. In fact, both surveys came across many cases in which children with polio walked to school on their hands and knees. Rather, they are prevented from enrolling in school in the first place by parents who are overprotective or do not see the point of investing in education for a child who is "not normal". Others drop out because they are unable to follow the curriculum in the absence of teachers who know Braille or sign language. The evidence presented in the livelihoods chapter tells the same story. It is not the individual impairment that excludes millions of disabled Indians from workplaces everywhere. Even a person with multiple disabilities has numerous abilities for which he or she could be employed. It is the perception of many employers that disabled people are an undesirable burden, unable to work as well as others, which prevents the disabled from even getting the chance to prove that this is not so. The chapter on social exclusion too shows that it is not the medical impairment, but the way in which society reacts to it, that excludes disabled villagers from taking part in celebrations, in political decision-making or religious worship. It is not that a blind person is incapable of getting married and having a family. It is the fact that few people would choose to marry a blind person in a village setting where the majority of marriages are arranged and bargained over. Disabled villagers do not constantly stay hidden behind the four walls of their home because they enjoy limited space so much. They do so because they run the risk of being reminded that they are not "normal" and that their disability is evidence of a sin committed in a former life whenever they go outside. So, the evidence presented in this book shows that the medical model does not adequately capture the reality of what it means to be disabled.

This is not to say that an impairment *per se* does not cause any problems and that all problems faced by disabled people stem from negative social attitudes. Indeed, Coleridge (2000) rightly points out that "the social model cannot be used to the complete exclusion of the medical model" (p. 26) and that deafness is usually a barrier regardless of the surrounding attitudes. Nonetheless, social attitudes are the main cause of the systematic exclusion of disabled people from all spheres of life and that the medical model does not capture this crucial aspect of disability.

These findings support the paradigm shift that is currently ongoing among disability groups in India from the medical model to the so-called *social model*. This model locates the cause of disability not in the bad health of the individual, but in disabling institutions, environments and attitudes. Disabling institutions include employers who do not consider disabled applicants or teachers who do not facilitate the learning of disabled children. Disabling environments prevent the participation of disabled people in all walks of life due to badly designed buildings or inaccessible transport. Disabling attitudes encompass any negative views of disability, such as the belief that disability is a bad omen. Far from being considered passive and helpless, the locus of control in the social model lies with disabled people themselves. Interventions are not targeted at helping the individual to adapt better to society's norms, but emphasise that society needs to change and remove the disabling institutions, environmental and attitudinal barriers that exclude the disabled.

From the social model of disability it is not far to the *rights-based approach* to disability, which locates its cause in the denial of basic human rights to disabled people. It sees the educational, social and economic disadvantage of disabled people as arising from the fact that disabled people have been denied the rights that other persons enjoy, including the right to a life of dignity with access to education and work. Rather than providing charity and welfare measures which make disabled people dependent, the rights-based approach emphasise empowerment and the provision of equal opportunities (Arora 2003). Not only is it important that society at large recognises that human rights apply to all human beings without distinction, but also that access is provided to the opportunities and resources required to realise these rights.

Defining Social Exclusion

Social exclusion has been defined as "the process through which individuals or groups are wholly or partially excluded from full participation in the society within which they live" (European Foundation cited in De Haan 2001: 26). The emphasis here is on process, for social exclusion is an inherently dynamic concept depicting the developments that lead to the state of being excluded. Social exclusion is also a relational concept in that it refers to the relationship of the individual with society and with the state. Just like disability social exclusion is a relative concept which is context specific and refers to someone being excluded from something in a particular time and place.

Exclusion has as many different dimensions as there are answers to the question "Excluded from what?" People can be excluded from health services, from education, from work, from places of worship, from social circles, from political bodies, from private or public celebrations, from citizenship and many other processes, institutions, groups, privileges, events, relationships and other domains that people can participate in. As different as these dimensions of exclusion may be, all of them have one thing in common – they all have social consequences.

Take for example economic exclusion. Exclusion from the paid labour market, which has traditionally been seen as the main aspect of social exclusion (cf. Barnes and Mercer 2003), does not only have economic consequences, but also impacts on the excluded person's status and role in society. In other words, exclusion from the labour market has consequences for that person's participation in many other spheres of life, for example family and community life. This is born out by the survey results discussed in this book which illustrate how lack of gainful employment can be both a barrier to marriage as well as a cause for its breakdown. The breakdown of marriage in a communitarian rather than individualistic society like India often carries with it stigma which in turn has further consequences for participation in social life.

Just as economic exclusion has social consequences, so does political exclusion. Bhalla and Lapeyre (2004) rightly argue that political exclusion in many countries results less from restrictions in political rights than from the lack of political representation and influence of the excluded. The excluded lack political influence because there is no representation of their specific interests that would make them a political force. The social consequence of such political exclusion is twofold. Firstly, the lack of political representation may translate into a lack of policies and programmes targeted towards the excluded. And, secondly, political exclusion may in some cases even have an impact on their access to social services like health and education.

These examples demonstrate why the concept of social exclusion refers to exclusion in the economic and political spheres as well as that in the strictly "social" sphere. It is because even in these spheres, which may at first sight appear unrelated, exclusion has social consequences. If integration, the opposite of exclusion, is defined as full participation in society, it is not hard to see why full participation in social relations would also require economic or political participation. Therefore a book about disability and social exclusion needs to examine exclusion from livelihoods as much as exclusion from marriage to be able to draw a complete picture of the social exclusion of disabled people in rural India.

The examples above further show that exclusion on one dimension may lead to further exclusion on another and so on whereby disadvantages on one dimension create or reinforce disadvantages on another until a person is excluded from multiple dimensions at the same time. In the final culmination of a series of exclusions it is sometimes hard to say which particular exclusion had caused the cumulative effect of the series. At the same time, this dynamic nature of the process of social exclusion is also an opportunity for combating it – if one exclusion, say that from the labour market, could be tackled, this would have beneficial consequences for the other dimensions too.

This is particularly true for disability in rural India. If, for example, the exclusion of poor people from quality healthcare could be overcome, many disabilities could be prevented (this is discussed in more depth in the medical chapter) and the consequent exclusion from education and livelihoods would thus be short-circuited.

Social Exclusion and Disability

Social exclusion is a key dimension in understanding what it means to be disabled in rural India. While disability can be understood as a static notion like poverty,[5] the social exclusion that results from it or indeed caused the disability in the first place is a dynamic process. And it is the participation and social relations aspect of this process, the actual experience of being excluded, which defines what it means to be disabled as much if not more than the physical experience of disability itself. Similarly, in a situation where all medical options have been exhausted, disabled people may be able to tackle the social exclusion associated with the state of being disabled to a greater extent than they may be able to tackle the disability itself.

While the previous section was mainly concerned with the "exclusion from what" question, relating social exclusion to disability requires taking a closer look at who is excluded. Disability is of course not the only answer to the question "exclusion of whom?" Traditionally, social exclusion has been defined with reference primarily to the working and unemployed poor. Indeed, the concept of social exclusion has been described as a successor to the US term "underclass" (ILO 1996). However, over time, as the concept of social exclusion gained popularity, it has also been used to understand the processes which lead to the marginalisation of other groups. International institutions like the European Council and the ILO have broadened the social exclusion debate by analysing how it relates to gender.[6] Social exclusion has also been discussed in the context of race, not least by the Social Exclusion Unit of the British government.

How then, if at all, does social exclusion on the basis of poverty, gender or race differ from social exclusion on grounds of disability? The survey findings discussed in this book suggest that disabled people in rural India are often excluded from education, livelihoods, medical care and social life. But so are people from lower castes and poor people in rural India and in particular the girls and women among them. Poor people too may be unable to send their children to school or afford a good doctor. They too may find it hard to find a decent husband for their daughter without being able to pay a dowry.

The difference is that disability adds additional barriers to full participation and thus exacerbates other causes of exclusion. Take for example education. Your chances of going to school may be slim if your family requires your daily wages for its survival. But they are virtually non-existent if your family required your wages for survival and you would be unable to follow class in any case because you are deaf and the teacher does not know sign language. For, in this instance, you would still not be able to go to school even if the wage constraint could somehow be overcome. Another example is marriage. A poor family may not be able to pay a competitive dowry but may be able to marry off their daughter anyway to men who do not command significant dowries. The parents of a poor disabled girl, on the other hand, will find it much harder to find a suitable and willing match, because they have to overcome not only the dowry problem, but also the stigma attached to disability. The chapter on social life provides ample evidence of this. It shows that in rural Rajasthan a lower percentage of disabled women are married compared to the general population, while the incidence of divorce is higher amongst disabled women. The case studies from the Andhra survey suggest that the only people willing to marry a disabled person tend to be widowed, suffer from chronic diseases, live in acute poverty or are looking for a second wife.

It is important at this point to keep in mind that social exclusion is a relative concept. The particular context of this discussion is not just disability in India, but particularly disability in rural India. Disability probably complicates participation in any country, but it does not necessarily constitute a complete barrier to participation. There are countries where most disabled children go to school every morning just like their non-disabled peers. There are countries where disabled people work in normal companies as well as in sheltered workshops earning their own income. There are countries in which disabled people get all the aids and appliances and correctional surgery they need. The experience of social exclusion on grounds of disability will be very different in these countries. The experience can be very different even in India itself, for example, for a disabled child in Mumbai, who has access to an integrated school of the Spastics Society of India. And the experience of disability today in any country is likely to be very different from the experience of disability in that country a hundred years ago. This is precisely the point of this book – to understand how and why the participation of disabled people in all spheres of life in rural India is limited still today, when the experience of other countries and indeed other areas in India shows that disability is not a barrier to participation that cannot be surmounted over time.

Role of the State

What role the Indian state has to play in removing the present barriers to the participation of disabled people in rural society depends entirely on the conception of social exclusion adopted. For different paradigms are based on different notions of who does the excluding with different implications for the role of the state. This section takes a look at the main paradigms of social exclusion to establish which one captures both disability and the Indian context best. It draws on Hilary Silver's three paradigms of social exclusion (cited for example in De Haan 2001), which are the most widely accepted formulation of the main approaches to social exclusion.

The first of the paradigms formulated by Silver is the so-called *solidarity* paradigm and is firmly rooted in the French republican tradition drawing on Rousseau which emphasises the idea of the state embodying the general will of the nation (cf. De Haan 2001). The social order is constructed around a "moral community" based on a core of shared values and rights (ILO 1996). A variety of institutions of the welfare state provide the mechanisms for integrating individuals in society. Exclusion is a rupture of the social fabric, a breakdown of the bond between the individual and society and as such is the result of the failure of the institutions of the state to integrate the individual.

Renee Lenoir, then French State Secretary of Social Action, is credited to have been the first to have used the term "social exclusion" (De Haan 2001). In 1974 he used the term to describe a wide range of excluded people, such as the poor, those with a physical or mental handicap, substance abusers, suicidal persons, the aged and other socially disadvantaged groups. Lenoir's view of the excluded was stigmatising in that he defined the excluded as marginal people, i.e., those who somehow did not fit the norms of industrial society.

However, this first definition of social exclusion evolved in the following decade in France to take on the meaning that is now associated with the solidarity paradigm. In the 1980s the term "social exclusion" became popular in France when it was used to capture the new social problems arising from economic restructuring and the crisis of the welfare state during that period. It concerned first and foremost those affected by these socioeconomic structural changes, for example those who had become unemployed, and did not define the excluded on the grounds of their personal characteristics as Lenoir had done. "The new poverty problem [in the France of the 1980s] did not pertain to the disabled or those excluded from social norms, but to an increasing proportion of the population suffering from such multidimensional problems as precarious jobs and long-term unemployment, the weakening of family and extra-family social networks and loss of social status" (Bhalla and Lapeyre 2004: 4).

This shift in the notion of social exclusion – from focusing on individuals, who had always been excluded and marginalised, to individuals, who had previously been well integrated into society but had lost their jobs or social status as a result of changes in economic policy – goes hand in hand with shifting blame onto the welfare state. It is because the state's old welfare policies were proving incapable of dealing with the new social problems arising in France during the 1980s that the resulting social exclusion was seen as owing to the failure of the state. It is this context which explains why the solidarity paradigm essentially assigns the responsibility to facilitate integration and prevent social exclusion to the state.

Silver's second paradigm is called the *specialisation* paradigm and is rooted in Anglo-Saxon liberal individualism. In this paradigm society is viewed as an amalgamation of free individuals who interact on the basis of voluntary choices in contractual exchanges governed by rights and duties. In this setting exclusion may result from a number of causes. "Individuals may exclude themselves by their choices, may be excluded because of the patterns of interest or contractual relationships among other actors, or their exclusion may occur as a result of discrimination, or market failures or of unenforced rights" (ILO 1996: 2). Since exclusion is seen as the outcome of voluntary interactions of individuals, the state, unlike in the French solidarity paradigm, is not responsible for exclusion and consequently has no role to play in combating it.

The third paradigm is called the *monopoly* paradigm and is rooted in Weber's theory of social closure and has been influential particularly in Northern European countries (De Haan 2001). Social exclusion is the consequence of group monopolies in a social order that is dominated by a hierarchy of power relations. So-called insiders monopolise resources to their advantage and erect barriers to restrict the access of outsiders through social closure. Inequality often overlaps with group identities determining who is excluded from what. "These inequalities are mitigated by 'social democratic citizenship' which when implemented will result in those who have been systematically excluded being able to actively participate in the contemporary society in which they live" (Lang 2002: 19).

The role of the state in fighting exclusion is very different in all these paradigms given the difference in the causes of exclusion identified in each. The solidarity paradigm assigns the state the biggest role of all three paradigms, because it defines exclusion as a direct consequence of the failure of the institutions of the state whose responsibility is to integrate the individual in society. The specialisation paradigm assigns no role to the state in combating exclusion as it defines exclusion as the outcome of voluntary contractual relationships between individuals. And the monopoly paradigm assigns a role to the state in so far as social democratic citizenship is seen as a way of overcoming exclusion and facilitating participation. The state thus has the responsibility to ensure that the social democratic citizenship of the excluded is upheld and to maintain a social democratic environment in which citizenship really can be a means of overcoming exclusion.

So, the role of the state differs by choice of paradigm. In order to understand what role the Indian state has to play in overcoming the exclusion of disabled people, we therefore need to take a closer look at which of these paradigms best captures the Indian context.

The solidarity paradigm would appear to capture the Indian reality least because it was defined in relation to a particular problem in a particular place and time, i.e., the emergence of the new poor following economic restructuring in France in the 1980s. The solidarity paradigm thus describes exclusion on the basis of unemployment by people who had previously been well integrated in society. This is very different from exclusion on the basis of disability. Furthermore, the solidarity paradigm defines exclusion as the outcome of the failure of the institutions of the state to integrate the newly poor into society. Recall that this notion is firmly rooted in French republicanism where the state is the embodiment of the general will of the nation which has the role to protect the social order constructed around a moral community based on shared values and rights. This is very different from the Indian context where it could be argued that the state governs a variety of communities, some of whom have different rights[7] and different values. The Indian state has failed to integrate a vast number of groups into society since its inception, and has certainly failed not only to prevent the emergence of the new poor and their consequent exclusion from society, but to combat the exclusion of the old poor too.

The specialisation paradigm too does not adequately capture exclusion on the basis of disability. Recall that the specialisation paradigm sees exclusion as a result of individuals excluding themselves by their voluntary choices, as a result of patterns of interest or contractual relationships among other actors and as a result of discrimination, market failures or unenforced rights. Apart from discrimination, none of these dimensions capture adequately the experience of being excluded on the basis of disability, for this is not the result of voluntary exclusion on the basis of personal choice and has nothing to do with the contractual relationships of others or indeed with market failure. The Anglo-Saxon liberalism that the specialisation paradigm draws on, which absolves the state from any responsibility in promoting integration, is not an adequate description of the Indian context. For example, the Indian state has put measures in place that are aimed at facilitating the integration of some historically excluded groups, such as reserving seats in the institutions of higher education and in the civil services for dalits. The specialisation paradigm therefore neither applies to exclusion on the basis of disability nor to the Indian state.

The monopoly paradigm captures both disability and the Indian context better than the specialisation and solidarity paradigms. Recall that the monopoly paradigm sees exclusion as a result of insider groups monopolising resources to their advantage and restricting access to outsiders. Recall too that inequality often overlaps with group identities and the consequent patterns of exclusion. Nothing could describe exclusion on the basis of disability in India better. In the monopoly paradigm outsiders are those who are denied access to certain economic and social opportunities and to participation in certain groups. They are often those who are already disadvantaged in one way or the other. This is precisely what is happening to disabled people in rural India, as the ensuing chapters in this book will illustrate. Already disadvantaged through their disability, disabled people find themselves excluded from school, where the non-disabled population monopolises all the resources, be it the time of teachers or the funding. Disabled people further find themselves excluded from panchayats or village governing bodies, where non-disabled people monopolise the membership and decision-making and consequently control the resources of those bodies. Disabled people in rural India also find themselves excluded from the workplace, where even non-disabled people often struggle to find gainful employment and therefore have an incentive to keep outsiders out. Some of the case studies in this book describe how non-disabled people have even attempted to monopolise places of worship and restrict access of disabled people there.

A paradigm that is grounded in a view of society dominated by group monopolies structured in a hierarchy of power relations has particular relevance in the Indian context. India is known for its group identities placing the individual in communities based on caste, family lineage, religion etc. And India is also known for the hierarchical nature of its social order. That the groups which dominate the hierarchy should protect the resources they control from outsiders is a natural outcome in this particular context. In a country like India the competition over scarce resources is fiercer than in many other countries simply on the basis of an imbalance between demand and supply. As more people than anywhere but in China are vying for fewer resources it is natural that insiders should be struggling to hang on to their advantages and defend their position to a growing number of outsiders.

So, the monopoly paradigm captures both the experience of exclusion on the basis of disability as well as the Indian context very well. What then does this mean for the role of the Indian state as implied by this monopoly paradigm? Recall that this paradigm sees social democratic citizenship as a means of overcoming exclusion. The state thus has a responsibility both to ensure that the social democratic citizenship of the excluded is upheld, i.e., that they are not denied certain rights, and to maintain a social democratic environment in which citizenship really can be a means of overcoming exclusion.

This means that it is the state's obligation to see to it that the legal rights guaranteed on paper are translated into practice. This involves providing adequate, timely and affordable healthcare not just to disabled people, but also to the population at large so that the 50 per cent of preventable disabilities[8] could actually be prevented. It further involves providing barrier-free schools with teachers who know how to facilitate learning of both non-disabled and disabled children. In addition, the state must act on preventing discrimination in the workplace or elsewhere on grounds of disability. The chapters of this book go into much greater depth in analysing the state's current policies and the scope for their improvement. Suffices it to say here that the policy recommendations in this book are grounded on a firm belief that it is not a charitable gesture, but the state's obligation to ensure that 50 million of its citizens are not denied the most basic of human rights.

Survey Methodology

The objective of the surveys was to comprehend the issues and problems that disabled people in rural India, and in particular the poorest among them, face in all spheres of life by collecting extensive quantitative and qualitative data from people from various regions and with different types of disability. The aim was to listen to the voices of these disabled people in order to understand their perspective of the various problems encountered during their life cycle. The surveys were carried out to investigate what factors bar disabled people in Indian villages from exercising such basic human rights as the right to education or the right to a life of dignity. They were to assess the programmatic response of the state to the identified issues and problems and ascertain the views of disabled villagers and their caregivers as to how their needs might be served better. The latter was of particular interest since the government of Andhra Pradesh had commissioned the survey with a view to formulating a state disability action plan and the Rajasthan State Disability Department was also interested in using the survey findings to prepare an action plan for improving the state's existing welfare schemes for disabled people.

The Andhra Pradesh survey covered 1,843 disabled people in 41 villages in 24 mandals[9] from 16 districts. The Rajasthan survey canvassed 1,021 disabled individuals in 50 villages in 12 blocks[10] from six districts. The types of disability covered included locomotor disability, visual impairment, speech and hearing impairment, mental retardation, mental illness, leprosy and multiple disability.

In Andhra Pradesh, the sample villages were selected through multi-stage purposive sampling for each of the state's three sub-regions, i.e., Telangana, Rayalaseema and Coastal Andhra. The database was comprised of all the secondary data available for the districts, mandals and villages in Andhra Pradesh, including data from the 1991 census,[11] the Village Directory, from the Panchayat Raj Departments at district level and from the Department of Economics and Statistics. From this database a weighted average of a number of socio-economic indicators was composed for the districts and mandals in each sub-region. The indicators that were chosen as variables for the weighted average of each district were number of villages affected by fluoride, number of disabled people, budget allocated in 2001-2002, scheduled caste population, scheduled tribe population, number of non-workers,[12] percentage of illiterates and percentage of female illiterates. For the classification of mandals the last five of these indicators were chosen. The districts and mandals were then both ranked by their respective weighted averages, and from this the districts to be studied were selected first, followed by the mandals to be studied within those districts. Since one of the study's aims was to understand the situation of the disabled among the rural poor, mandals were selected with a bias towards backward areas as represented in low averages. Once 24 mandals had thus been selected from 16 districts from amongst the three sub-regions, the villages to be studied were chosen from these mandals with a view to including all types of disability as well as different population groups such as fisherfolk and tribals. Table 1.1 below lists the 41 villages finally selected in Andhra Pradesh.

Table 1.1
Villages Covered by the Andhra Pradesh Survey

	Village	*Mandal*	*District*
1.	Koragam	Burja	Srikakulam
2.	Peddapeta	Burja	Srikakulam
3.	Sambham	Seethampeta	Srikakulam
4.	Baguvalasa	Garividi	Vizianagaram
5.	Bondapalle	Garividi	Vizianagaram
6.	Annavaram	Bheemunipatnam	Visakhapatnam
7.	Vanthalamamidi	Paderu	Visakhapatnam
8.	Vadanarsapuram	Rambilli	Visakhapatnam
9.	Nellore Rural (1)	Nellore	Nellore
10.	Penubarthi	Rapur	Nellore
11.	Yepuru	Rapur	Nellore
12.	Bingini Palle	Singaraya Konda	Prakasam
13.	Pakala	Singaraya Konda	Prakasam
14.	Katikaparula Colony	Singaraya Konda	Prakasam
15.	Kamarupalle	Anantapur	Anantapur
16.	Obulapuram	Putlur	Anantapur
17.	Badikayalapalle	B.Kothakota	Chittoor
18.	Gattu	B.Kothakota	Chittoor
19.	Patha Manchuru	Vayalpad	Chittoor
20.	B.T. Nagar	Nandyal	Kurnool
21.	Bumanagireddipallie	Rudravaram	Kurnool
22.	Ellavathula	Rudravaram	Kurnool
23.	Machinenipalle	Rudravaram	Kurnool
24.	Malepadu	Yerraguntla	Cuddapah
25.	Nidizivve	Yerraguntla	Cuddapah
26.	Gowraram	Bayyaram	Khammam

Contd...

Contd...

27.	Mahanthipur	Bomraspeta	Mahbubnagar
28.	Kothapalle Thanda	Maddur	Mahbubnagar
29.	Thimmareddipalle	Maddur	Mahbubnagar
30.	Kanakamamidi	Moinabad	Rangareddi
31.	Kethireddipalle	Moinabad	Rangareddi
32.	Badgoni	Nadipet	Nizamabad
33.	Talveda	Nadipet	Nizamabad
34.	Kausalyadevipalle	Narsimhulapet	Warangal
35.	Vanthadupula	Narsimhulapet	Warangal
36.	Gaddikondaram	Thipparthi	Nalgonda
37.	Kankanala Palle	Thipparthi	Nalgonda
38.	Pajjur	Thipparthi	Nalgonda
39.	Salewada (Khurd)	Utnur	Adilabad
40.	Umri	Utnur	Adilabad
41.	Yenda	Utnur	Adilabad

In Rajasthan, one district was selected from each of the state's six administrative regions following consultations with the Social Welfare Department and the Disability Commissioner in the state. From these districts, the villages to be surveyed were selected randomly after being ranked on each of the following indicators: presence of a primary health centre or hospital in the village, presence of a school, scheduled caste population and scheduled tribe population. A list of the villages covered by the survey in Rajasthan is presented in Table 1.2.

The majority of the members of the research teams in both Rajasthan and Andhra Pradesh were drawn from amongst disabled people and from NGOs working in the realm of disability. A total of 65, out of 80 researchers in

Table 1.2
Villages Covered by the Rajasthan Survey

	Village	*Block*	*District*
1.	Mohanpura (8Y)	Ganganagar	Ganganagar
2.	4 ML	Ganganagar	Ganganagar
3.	6 DOL-A	Anupgarh	Ganganagar
4.	3 KNDA	Anupgarh	Ganganagar
5.	7 DOL-A	Anupgarh	Ganganagar
6.	5 G CHOTTI	Ganganagar	Ganganagar
7.	19 RJD	Anupgarh	Ganganagar
8.	20 RJD	Anupgarh	Ganganagar
9.	12 KND	Anupgarh	Ganganagar
10.	12 KPD	Anupgarh	Ganganagar
11.	Rajana	Garhi	Banswara
12.	Singla Kundi	Kushalgarh	Banswara
13.	Sarpota	Kushalgarh	Banswara
14.	Metwala	Garhi	Banswara
15.	Jharas	Garhi	Banswara
16.	Satalya Ki Todi	Kushalgarh	Banswara
17.	Kundiya	Kushalgarh	Banswara
18.	Birwani	Shahabad	Baran
19.	Pajantori	Shahabad	Baran
20.	Bamulya Mataji	Anta	Baran
21.	Uchavada	Shahabad	Baran
22.	Kirad Phadi	Shahabad	Baran
23.	Bijora	Anta	Baran
24.	Jhurli	Osian	Jodhpur
25.	Khari Kala	Osian	Jodhpur
26.	Khari Khurd	Osian	Jodhpur

Contd...

Contd...

27.	Vishnu Nagar	Vishnu Nagar	Jodhpur
28.	Jetiwas	Osian	Jodhpur
29.	Lumbasar	Bap	Jodhpur
30.	Bangati Kala	Phalodi	Jodhpur
31.	Miyakour	Bap	Jodhpur
32.	Dabri	Ladnu	Nagaur
33.	Chandrai	Ladnu	Nagaur
34.	Nundra	Makrana	Nagaur
35.	Dewla	Makrana	Nagaur
36.	Heerawati	Ladnu	Nagaur
37.	Rampura	Makrana	Nagaur
38.	Bhaiya Khurd	Makrana	Nagaur
39.	Taj Kha Ka Bas	Chaksu	Jaipur
40.	Bamanpura	Chaksu	Jaipur
41.	Balmukandpura	Chaksu	Jaipur
42.	Itawa Bhopchi	Chomu	Jaipur
43.	Nivana	Chomu	Jaipur
44.	Rupadikalla	Chaksu	Jaipur
45.	Sampatpura	Chaksu	Jaipur
46.	Mandeliya	Chaksu	Jaipur
47.	Antpura	Chomu	Jaipur
48.	Narothampura	Chaksu	Jaipur
49.	Baghvatserkankeria	Chaksu	Jaipur
50.	Bhalai Basthi	Jaipur	Jaipur

Andhra Pradesh and 42 out of the 48 researchers in Rajasthan were disabled. The survey teams included researchers with different types of disability, including locomotor, hearing and visual impairment. Several researchers especially learned sign language for the survey work.

The members of the survey teams were trained in research techniques, including participatory tools and case study methods, during two weeks of capacity building, where they also shared their own experiences and understanding of disability in rural India with each other. Among others, this training was facilitated in Andhra Pradesh by Dr Murthy and Dr Sekar from the National Institute for Mental Health and Neurosciences (NIMHANS), India.

The research was participatory in several ways. Firstly, as was noted above, disabled people participated significantly in carrying out the survey. Secondly, the design of the study was developed in close consultation with disabled people. The initial questionnaire draft was field tested by the survey team in six villages in Andhra Pradesh and modified accordingly before the full survey was administered. In Rajasthan, the same survey design was modified once again with the help of disabled people there to fit local conditions. Thirdly, the research tools were participatory, as will be discussed below.

Teams of five researchers spent a minimum of five days in each village, during which they carried out Participatory Rural Appraisals (PRAs), administered a survey questionnaire and recorded case studies. Each member of the research team stayed in the home of a family of a disabled person for the duration of the survey in that village. This was done to ensure that the issues examined in the survey were understood from the point of view of the disabled persons and their caregivers. After an initial introduction to the village, typically by the village sarpanch, the research team would explain the purpose of their visit as well as the survey process to the assembled village community. In some villages such formal meetings were replaced with singing songs and painting wall-writings and placards about the survey with the help of school teachers and young people in the village.

The next step was to gain the support and cooperation of the local disabled people to be surveyed and motivate them to participate in a study that did not reward them with any immediate direct benefits. In many villages the researchers were met with open cynicism, owing to negative past experiences with other governmental and non-governmental studies. "Everybody comes, writes down something, makes big promises but ultimately gives nothing" was a typical first reaction by many disabled villagers. A lot of effort went into visiting people's houses and workplaces to convince them to participate. Special emphasis in rapport building was given to scheduled and backward caste[13] areas and minority hamlets[14] to ensure that the most vulnerable disabled people would be covered by the survey. The support of local NGOs as well as the fact that the majority of researchers could introduce themselves as being "fellow disabled persons" motivated a large number of people to participate in the end. This enabled the disabled researchers to collect quantitative and qualitative data usually not disclosed by the villagers due to their distrust of outside researchers.

After introduction to the village and rapport building, the next task ahead was to ascertain the number of disabled people in the village, along with the type of disability and the location of their houses. When initially asked how many disabled people lived in their village, villagers typically answered, "hardly three to four". The villagers were very surprised to see how many more disabled people were "discovered" in the consequent identification process. This process identified disabled people through multiple sources, including a door-to-door survey, social mapping of the village by disabled people and key village residents, visits to the school and Anganwadi centres[15] as well as discussions with shopkeepers and the leaders of different castes. Throughout this process the researchers tried to facilitate identification of disabled people by making villagers aware of the different types and symptoms of disability with pictures, role plays and even by referring to local nicknames of different disabilities.

Once the introduction, rapport building and identification of potential survey respondents had been successfully completed, the actual survey work of collecting quantitative and qualitative data through PRAs, questionnaires and case studies could begin. PRAs were carried out with various groups, some consisting of disabled people only, others including also their caregivers and other stakeholders such as teachers or ANM workers.[16] Different PRA methods were used to ascertain different issues. For example, the awareness of and access to government schemes for disabled people was assessed with a cobweb analysis. A matrix was used to understand disabled people's access to the existing livelihood opportunities in and around the village. Barriers to education, livelihood opportunities, medical care and social exclusion were discussed using a venn diagram. Case studies were collected through extensive discussions with disabled people and with their carers, sometimes even staying with the families. In addition, a door-to-door survey questionnaire was administered to the identified disabled people. In Andhra Pradesh, this survey contained 19 questions, which was expanded to 68 questions in Rajasthan.

In a review of the Andhra Pradesh survey, Werner (2002) noted that both survey design and process were "remarkably creative and socio-culturally appropriate" (p. 4). "The full involvement/employment/leadership of disabled persons as the main actors in every aspect of the process makes this analytic survey developed by ActionAid a groundbreaking approach which, in my belief, makes it a model that deserves wide attention and dissemination" (ibid.). We have seen above that the survey quality was greatly enhanced by the participation of disabled researchers, as they were able to collect rare and sensitive data usually not disclosed by villagers for distrust of outsiders. What is more, the participatory nature of the survey did not only benefit the survey, but also the surveyors and the people surveyed. In Werner's words, the survey process had been "a rewarding and empowering process for the disabled interviewers as well as for the disabled persons they had interviewed" (ibid.).

Indeed, the survey training and exposure benefited the participants far beyond the survey, with activities continuing to this day, long after the survey is over. Many of the disabled people involved in the Andhra Pradesh survey have come together and formed a "Network of Persons with Disability" in the state, which had reached a membership of 10,000[17] by the year 2004. Some disabled researchers initiated their own small projects to address some of the problems encountered during the research. Thirupathamma, a locomotor disabled woman from Medak district in Andhra Pradesh, said that the survey had opened her eyes: "I realised while talking to countless other disabled women in the many villages we surveyed that the problems I myself was experiencing as a disabled woman in my own village were not unique to me, but the common fate of many. I was shocked to see the extent of discrimination and wanted to do something to help".[18] So Thirupathamma went back to her district, which had not been covered by the survey, and started several disabled women's self-help groups. She said that the survey training and process had given her the necessary confidence and taught her how to lead a group discussion and encourage people to participate.

Limitations of the Survey

It is a tremendously challenging task to survey the phenomenon of disability in rural India given the different types of disability, the enormous regional spread and differences within each region. It is important to note the limitations that arise in this context.

Despite the enormous motivation and sensitivity of the researchers, the intensive nature of the survey and the multiple sources and methods of identification used, the survey team could barely identify half of the disabled people believed to exist in each village. While it is reasonable to expect that 5 per cent of the total population are disabled (cf. discussion above) the surveys found hardly half this number. In rural Rajasthan, 1,021 persons with disabilities were identified and administered the survey questionnaire, which is 1.4 per cent of the total population of 75,260 in the areas surveyed. In rural Andhra Pradesh, the survey located 1,843 disabled people in an area with a total population of 73,195, which amounts to 2.5 per cent. Even as the survey teams were leaving the villages after finishing their investigations, more disabled people were discovered. So deep is the social invisibility of disabled villagers that even these highly participatory and intensive surveys could not identify all disabled people.

A further limitation is that the surveys perhaps do not adequately represent the concerns of villagers with speech and hearing or mental disabilities. While some of the researchers had learned sign language to facilitate communication with the former, they had learned Hindi sign language, which was of little use in the Telugu-speaking villages of Andhra Pradesh. So, in practice, the surveyors largely relied on the carers when interviewing persons with speech and hearing disability to provide answers to the questionnaire, whose views may not be synonymous with those of the disabled person. The same was true for persons with mental disability, whose views and case studies were largely represented by their carers.

Composition of Samples

With respect to the *gender* division of the survey samples, 42 per cent of disabled persons surveyed in rural Andhra Pradesh and 37 per cent in rural Rajasthan were women. The *age* composition of the samples is as follows: in Rajasthan, 23 per cent of the sample was below 15 years of age, 42 per cent were between 15 and 35 years, 30 per cent were between 35 and 60 years and 5 per cent were older than 60. In Andhra Pradesh, the distribution was 25 per cent, 41 per cent, 29 per cent and 4 per cent respectively. Disability affects all age groups: cataract, for example, affects mainly people over 40 years, while cerebral palsy and polio are largely pre-school diseases.

The distribution of the sample by *type of disability* shows the same order of different types of disability by size in the samples of both states. Persons with locomotor disability form by far the largest group, followed by persons with speech and hearing impairment, and visually impaired persons. In

Figure 1.1
Distribution of Disabled Persons Surveyed in Andhra Pradesh by Type of Disability

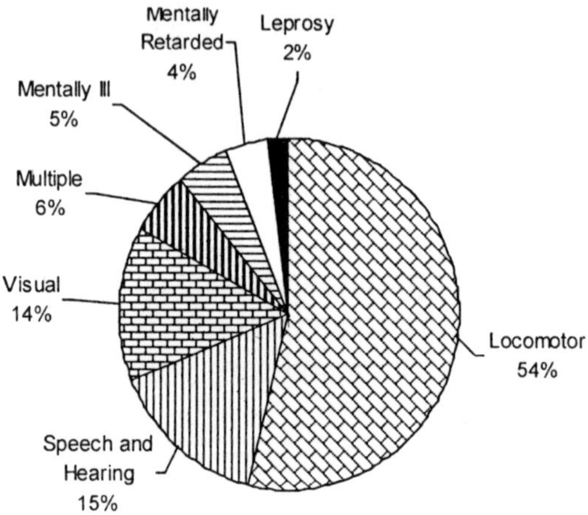

both states there are more persons with mental illness than with mental retardation and these two groups in turn exceed the number of persons with leprosy. Figure 1.1 shows the distribution of disabled persons surveyed by type of disability for Andhra Pradesh. The distribution almost exactly mirrors the distribution found for the whole of rural India by the NSSO (2003). While the order of the different types of disability by size is the same in Rajasthan as in Andhra Pradesh, the proportions differ slightly. In Rajasthan 61 per cent of disabled people surveyed had locomotor disabilities, followed by 11 per cent with speech and hearing impairment, 10 per cent with visual impairment, 8 per cent with mental illness, 5 per cent with multiple disabilities, 4 per cent with mental retardation and 2 per cent affected by leprosy.

Chapter Outline

This book attempts to document the voices of disabled people in rural India. It is organised around four major issues which disabled villagers face at different stages of their lives: medical care, education, livelihoods, and social exclusion. The chapters on each of these issues begin with a quantitative and qualitative description of the present situation, then analyse the various factors which create this situation and depict the consequences of this state of affairs. This is then complemented with an analysis of the government's response and conclude with suggestions for policy improvements and a delineation of the scope for civil society action. Secondary literature is used throughout the chapters to place the primary data into context.

Together, the chapters illustrate the vicious cycle of marginalisation and systematic exclusion of disabled people in all spheres of life, which begins and ends with social exclusion. The negative attitudes and misconceptions of disability cause disabled people to be hidden away in their own homes. Being hidden in turn causes isolation, loneliness and silence on the part of the disabled, as a result of which disability as a phenomenon becomes invisible. The invisibility of their problems causes voicelessness on the part of disabled people, which is why they remain by and large unnoticed despite their significant numbers. And voicelessness explains the lack of attention from the state and society to their reality and concerns. It explains why the difficulties facing disabled people at all stages in their life continue to receive only scant attention and why nothing is done to ameliorate their situation. By making some of the issues and concerns of disabled people in far away villages visible, this book hopes to take one step towards breaking out of this vicious cycle.

Playing with coloured marbles, Manjunath can pass off for any child in Meghalpallya village in Karnataka. Beaming fondly in welcome, he beckons with his hands to come and sit in his house. Only when he starts speaking, and that somewhat incoherently, does the realisation dawn that Manju, as he is fondly called, may not be like the other children after all.

Until the age of five Manju really had been a child like any other. His mother Sidhamma vividly remembers the ill-fated day that year when her child fell ill, never to be okay again. Manju all of a sudden had a fever, which did not subside for thirteen days despite frequent visits to doctors in the nearest town Y.N. Hosakota. Seeing that these doctors could not help and believing that the fever was the influence of some bad soul on their son, Manju's parents next took him to the traditional healer. Along with an ayurvedic doctor who frequented the village, the healer judged Manju's condition to be grave. Both demanded heavy fees for their attempts to heal the child, which Manju's father Hanumantappa, a daily wage labourer, could not meet from his meager income but covered by indebting himself with the moneylender. When none of the healer's efforts showed any effect and failed to halt the deteriorating condition of the child, the healer simply disappeared, while Manju's parents worked tirelessly to service the debt they had accumulated in the process.

When the fever finally subsided, Manju was not the same anymore. It took his parents some time to come to terms with the fact that Manju was now a '*mand-budhhi*', a child with mental retardation. Once the family recovered from the shock, they sent Manju back to

Contd. on next page...

school. He had been a good and active student before the illness, and since there were no special schools around, his parents assumed that Manju would continue to get educated in his old school, taking his own time. Yet his teachers thought otherwise. In the beginning they complained of Manju's inability to learn and keep pace with the other children of the same class. There were repeated efforts by the teachers to force Manju's parents to withdraw their child. When the parents refused, Manju was made an errand boy of the class, and was made to fetch water for other pupils, sweep the floor and do other such errands instead of getting an education. He wasn't allowed to sit in the classroom anymore. His classmates soon followed the example set by their teachers and started ridiculing and verbally abusing Manju, who reacted by beating them up. When Manju's parents learned that their son had been reduced to being an errand's boy, they withdrew him from school.

His parents bought a cow to keep the child busy and thus prevent him from fighting with anyone. But that did not reconcile them to the village community, which had turned hostile. Their neighbours stopped eating at their house, saying that Manju was putting his dirty hands into the drinking water. Hanumantappa sadly explains that the social ostracism they are facing is one of the worst forms of contempt in the village. When asked what happens to children with mental retardation in a village, he replies, "Nothing, they just survive, dragging along their souls... As long as we live, we'll look after him. And once we are gone ..." His voice chokes and he leaves the sentence unfinished.

Notes

1. Apart from leaving out these types of disability, there are also other limitations of the NSSO methodology. Krishnaswamy (1987) argues that the sample selected for the estimation of the prevalence of disability is very small and has an urban bias, in that the representation of urban/rural households is not proportionate.
2. Own calculation from Statement 2, p. 9 in NSSO (2003). The estimated number of persons with any disability in that table is 14.085 million in rural India and 4.406 million in urban India.
3. The full name of the Act is "The Persons with Disabilities (Equal Opportunities, Protection of Rights and Full Participation) Act". It was passed by the Indian Parliament in 1995 and ratified by the President of India in 1996.
4. See Chart 2, p. 11 in NSSO (2003) for a ranking of states by incidence of disability.
5. This is not to say that disability is a static state that cannot change – the medical chapter discusses how various interventions can change a disability.
6. Apart from the European Council and the ILO, Scandinavian countries have placed particular importance on the gender dimension of social exclusion. During its presidency of the EU in 2002, the Danish government held a conference on gender and social exclusion and there are numerous research programmes of social exclusion and gender at Universities in Scandinavia.
7. For example, the difference in Hindu and Muslim civil law regarding marriage.
8. This figure is quoted in DFID (2000), p. 3.
9. A *mandal* is the smallest state defined development unit, encompassing on average 20 to 25 villages.
10. In Rajasthan, a mandal is called "block" and may also be referred to as taluka.
11. Detailed figures for the 2001 census were not yet available at that time.

12. *Non-workers* are defined in the Census of India as those persons who have not been employed for even one single day in a calendar year.
13. *Scheduled castes* are those at the bottom of or outside the caste hierarchy. They are called "scheduled" because they appeared in a list of socially deprived castes prepared by the British Government in 1935. *Backward castes* have a ritual rank and occupational status above Scheduled Castes and Scheduled Tribes but remain socially and economically depressed (cf. Human Rights Watch 1999).
14. A hamlet is a human settlement in rural areas that is situated within a legally recognised village.
15. An 'Anganwadi' is a state-run centre for early childhood care and protection.
16. ANM is short for Auxiliary Nurse Midwife, health assistants working in government-run primary health centres (PHCs).
17. Figure taken from a flyer distributed by the network at the 2004 World Social Forum in Mumbai.
18. Private communication on 20 March 2004 in Rachur village, Mahabubnagar district of Andhra Pradesh. She made this statement in Telugu.

2

MEDICAL CARE

Disability Prevention and Rehabilitation

The enormous problems that many villagers face in various spheres of life as a result of a disability as described in this book, underline the vital importance of access to timely and adequate medical care for it has the potential to avoid most of the problems described by preventing a disability in the first place or by lessening its impact. The case studies throughout this book illustrate that all misery began when the family failed to attain proper medical help and was left to deal with the unabated and never ending consequences of disability which manifest themselves everywhere: in school, at work, at home and in the village community. Medical care is therefore a crucial area of concern in addressing the dismal overall situation in which disabled people in rural India find themselves. This chapter therefore looks at the various aspects of disability prevention and rehabilitation as currently practised in India.

Disability prevention refers to the various medical measures taken to avert the causes of disability. Prevention is crucial in reducing the incidence of disability. Disability rehabilitation is the effort to integrate persons with disability into mainstream society. Until the late 1950s rehabilitation was understood merely as the physical management of a disability and was practised widely by institutionalising persons with disability in special institutions. But, in the 1970s, a shift towards community-based rehabilitation (CBR) took place, redefining rehabilitation as a holistic process of integrating disabled people into society with close involvement of the family and community. Rehabilitation is thus a wide term encompassing many different areas, including educational, occupational, social and psychological rehabilitation. This chapter is concerned with the medical aspects of rehabilitation, in particular with speech- and physiotherapy and aids and appliances.

While it is true that private providers play a major role in the delivery of health services in India, this chapter nevertheless focuses exclusively on the public health sector and does not analyse the private sector or indigenous systems of medicine. Voluntary health agencies are discussed only in so far as the state finances them to deliver its policy. This is both because the book sees the provision of public services as the responsibility of the state and also because it is concerned with the situation of poor persons with disability in Rajasthan and Andhra Pradesh. Poor people use private health services much less than those with higher incomes (cf. Table 9.1 in NHFS 2000) and the Millennial Survey of India's Public Services recently revealed that in poor states like Rajasthan government health services are the major source of healthcare for the majority of the population (PAC 2002).

Access and Quality of Health Services

For the majority of disabled people in rural India, *medical care is beyond reach.* While 80 per cent of the disabled live in rural areas, rehabilitative services are concentrated in urban areas (Alkazi 1992). Only 2 per cent of the disabled rural population have access to rehabilitative services (ibid.). In Andhra Pradesh, 60 per cent of the villages covered by PRAs had no doctor. In Rajasthan, 60 per cent of those who said they required corrective surgery had not been operated. Less than 7 per cent of disabled people surveyed in Andhra Pradesh and only 11 per cent in Rajasthan had received aids and appliances. Only 15 per cent of families surveyed in rural Andhra Pradesh had received assistance from an ANM[1] worker, a nurse who is responsible for attending to the basic health needs of the rural population. Only 10 per cent of hospitals distributed aids and appliances and none of them offered physiotherapy or counselling.

Medical care is beyond the reach of disabled villagers because it is beyond the reach of the rural population as a whole. The doctor-population ratio for India as a whole is 1:2000.[2] This average ratio is much worse for the rural areas, given the disparity of health manpower distribution between rural and urban areas, with a concentration of doctors up to 80 per cent in urban areas (Park 1998). There is one hospital bed for 2,347 people in Rajasthan (Pande 2003: 27). In 1995 only every third to fifth specialist position required in community health centres was actually filled, which means that only 29 per cent of surgeons, 24 per cent of physicians, 23 per cent of obstetricians and gynaecologists and 21 per cent of paediatricians needed were hired in community health centres.[3]

The Andhra Pradesh government spent only Rs 157 and the Rajasthan government only Rs 151[4] per person on health in 2002-03, which is less than what 18 other states and union territories spent during the same year. This expenditure is completely insufficient compared to actual costs of treatment. These encompass not just the payment to the doctor or hospital, necessary even in most government healthcare facilities, but also the costs incurred in the purchase of medicines, food and transport as well as any lost income. This is discussed in more detail below. Suffices it to say here that the per capita health expenditure is hardly enough to cover the actual costs incurred by the average patient, which amounted to Rs 582 per episode in a "free ward" of a rural hospital even back in 1987.[5] Villagers with disability, who have a much greater need for medical care, spent an average of Rs 1,200 per year on clinic visits in 1995.[6]

With such meagre per capita expenditure, it is perhaps not surprising that government healthcare services are generally of poor quality. Gopalan and Mishra (2000: 246) note that studies consistently show dissatisfaction with government health services due to rude and improper behaviour on the part of health staff, staff shortages, lack of supplies and drugs and long waits to see a doctor.

The Millennial Survey of India's Public Services (PAC 2002) is one such study which recorded notoriously low satisfaction rates and found that only 13 per cent of patients in Rajasthan and 29 per cent in Andhra Pradesh were fully satisfied with doctors and paramedical staff at government health facilities. Only 28 per cent of users in Andhra Pradesh reported that a doctor was present at the time of their visit to the government facility. 23 per cent of the inpatients in Andhra Pradesh even reported having to pay bribes to receive treatment. "The average *district hospital* is starved of funds even for basic consumables necessary for essential sterile precautions – linen, gloves, needles, syringes etc" (Sundararaman et al 1996: 24). The situation in the district hospitals is mirrored in the *primary health centres* (PHCs), which are the cornerstone of the rural healthcare system. A study of 398 PHCs from eighteen states undertaken by the Indian Council of Medical Research in 1989 found that only 12 per cent of these were capable of handling the recommended work (cited in Pande 2003). The Independent Commission on Health notes in its 1997 report that while in most states there is now one PHC per 30,000 people and one sub-centre (SC) per 5,000 people as envisaged in the 1983 National Health Policy,[7] the infrastructure is "grossly underutilised because of poor facilities, inadequate supplies, insufficient effective person-hours and lack of proper monitoring" (p.38). The Andhra Pradesh survey confirmed this. For example, Jangamala, a woman with multiple disabilities from Nandipeta mandal in Nizamabad district said that doctors hardly ever visited the primary health centre in her mandal. The survey also found that in some districts specialist doctors are not available even at the district headquarters, making it impossible for some disabled villagers to get the required treatment.

The Independent Commission on Health judged the community services provided by *ANM workers*, who visit the village once or twice a month, to be "sub-standard", owing to inadequate training, very poor supervision and guidance and shortage of medicines and equipment at the health centres (cf. p. 32). ANMs tend to focus entirely on pregnant women and do not attend to disabled people. The ANM workers interviewed in the Rajasthan and Andhra Pradesh surveys generally did not know how many disabled people lived in the village or what their disabilities were. Even in their work with expecting women, ANM workers did not seem to be aware of the importance of prenatal measures to prevent disability.

Similarly, *Anganwadi workers* are also not trained in measures of disability prevention among the people under their care. They are attached to the Integrated Child Development Scheme (ICDS), covering each a population of 1,000 in the 5,320 ICDS blocks in India. Ninety per cent of the ICDS projects are located in rural and tribal areas (RCI 2000). The Anganwadi worker receives training in health, nutrition and child development in order to attend to expecting and nursing mothers and pre-school children. Even though the ICDS is directed at a critical age group with respect to disability prevention, and immunisation is a key part of the responsibilities of an Anganwadi worker, "children with disabilities remain marginalized in the ICDS programme and its activities" (Bacquer and Sharma 1997: 115). A study by the National Institute of Nutrition found that 40-50 per cent of Anganwadi workers in Andhra Pradesh could not even distinguish children who were backward in their psychological development from those who developed normally (cited in ibid.).

Similar quality problems are found in the process of disability certification. Disability certificates attest the nature and extent of a given disability and are mandatory for availing benefits under government schemes for disabled people, such as conveyance allowance, travel concessions and tax deductions (Wadhwa 2002). Thus, the medical certification process has far reaching implications for many other spheres of life. According to the Persons with Disabilities Act, 1995, only a medical board constituted by the central and state governments can issue disability certificates. The certificates are issued during medical camps. The Andhra Pradesh survey found that disabled people were unaware of the dates of the camps, which are announced in newspapers. Camps were often held in distant places, and some villagers were told upon reaching the camp that in order to receive a certificate they had to go to district headquarters instead. Others were sent back home and told to come to a later camp, either because the doctors had failed to turn up or because not everyone could be certified in a one-day camp. In many hospitals the surveyors found that the equipment required for testing and certifying disability was not available, as was the case in Srikakulam district hospital, which lacked facilities to test speech and hearing impairment.

Aids and Appliances

Appropriate aids and appliances are an important aspect of physical rehabilitation. They play a crucial role in compensating for the loss of a particular body function. Technical aids can facilitate daily activities and lead to self-reliance, enabling a person with disability to carry out tasks that would have been impossible to do without the aid. For many disabled people, aids and appliances are just as important as corrective surgery or physiotherapy. Hearing aids can make a big difference to the hearing impaired, as can artificial limps to amputees, while callipers can enable a child with polio to walk and Braille slates help blind children to read. It has been shown, for example, that when hearing aids are fitted in children under six months, a large number of non-nuebella cases may regain hearing considerably (Alkazi 1992) and thus make a transition from a world of silence to the world of sound.

The Union Government provides free aids to needy physically disabled people under a scheme called "Assistance of Disabled Persons for Purchase/Fitting of Aids and Appliances", instituted in 1981 and administered by the Ministry of Social Justice and Empowerment. Aids and appliances up to a value of Rs 3,600 are distributed free of cost to persons with a monthly income of less than Rs 1,200, while those with an income of Rs 2,500 per month can buy the aids at 50 per cent of the price (cf. Appendix I in RCI 2000). The aids are manufactured and distributed by companies and NGOs.

In 1976, the Artificial Limbs Manufacturing Corporation (AMLICO) was set up in Kanpur as a public sector company to manufacture aids and appliances. It is now setting up four Auxiliary Production Centres to increase the production of wheelchairs and tricycles. Despite being heavily subsidised by the government, AMLICO was running into huge losses until 1999. The Planning Commission (2001:21) noted that further critical and persisting problems with AMLICO are the costliness of its products and the low acceptability among users.

In practice, the many benefits of aids and appliances are hardly realised. Recall from above that less than 7 per cent of persons with disability surveyed in Andhra Pradesh, and only 11 per cent in Rajasthan had received aids and appliances. Most of the aids received were of poor quality. The Rajasthan survey found that only 11 per cent of the disabled who obtained aids and appliances are actually using them, which amounts to a rejection rate of 89 per cent. The large majority stopped using them because of the poor quality of the aids, because they had not been trained in using them, or because the aids are unsuited to local conditions. A tricycle, for example, was discovered to be of no use in the sands of western Rajasthan or in the hilly terrain of Banswara. None of the sample villages had repair centres, as a result of which even minor damage renders the appliance useless to its disabled owner. In light of this, 40 per cent of persons with disability surveyed in Rajasthan resorted to making appliances themselves, mostly wooden crutches and blind sticks.

The high rejection rates of aids and appliances by patients recorded in the survey confirms earlier observations by Dr P.K. Sethi, the inventor of the "Jaipur foot", who found time and again that children with polio would abandon their callipers and prefer to crawl on their hands, limp or drag their bodies on the ground instead. This, argues Dr Sethi, reflects the flaw in the emphasis at the planning level to import Western technology, whose design, materials and production cost is completely inadequate in the Indian setting, especially in rural areas, and which consequently cause problems in purchase, distribution and maintenance (cited in Alkazi 1992: 391). The Western lower limb prosthesis, for example, was not at all suited to the needs of Indian amputees. Thomas (1991) explains that it was designed stiff at the ankle, to slip into a shoe, and did not resemble a human foot. In India, people wear either sandals or walk barefoot in hot weather and a prosthesis therefore needs to look like a proper foot. While the Western foot prosthesis only allows the user to sit on a chair, ankle mobility is necessary in a prosthesis in India, as most people in rural India sit cross-legged on the floor. These contextual inadequacies prompted Dr Sethi to develop the famous Jaipur foot, a rubber prosthesis that resembles a normal foot made of local, inexpensive materials.

Narayana's village is 100 km away from the headquarters of his district in Andhra Pradesh. He applied for a tricycle from the Assistant Director of the Disability Office. He had to go six times to that office, which is located at district headquarters, before the tricycle was finally sanctioned and spent nearly Rs 3,000 on travel expenses and the tricycle. When he returned to his village he found that the tricycle did not work properly on the village roads and he ultimately stopped using the tricycle after only two months.

Primary Disability Prevention

The survey findings discussed above reflect the medical needs of its disabled respondents, i.e., people who already have injuries, congenital conditions or diseases that cause impairments or disabilities. They require health services at the secondary or tertiary level of disability prevention. At the *secondary level* of prevention, medical interventions aim at preventing deformities, so that diseases and congenital conditions do not result in impairments[8] or disabilities[9]. For example, early anti-tuberculosis treatment can prevent tuberculosis of the spine from progressing to the paralytic stage. At the *tertiary level*, medical interventions aim to limit the consequences of impairments or disabilities. In polio cases, for example, callipers and corrective surgery could prevent contractures of hip, knees and ankles from restricting mobility.

But the role of medical services in disability prevention is not restricted to people who already have disease or injury and require corrective surgery, physiotherapy or aids and appliances to prevent this from developing into a disability, or to limit the extent of disability. Medical care also has a crucial role to play at the *primary level* of prevention, i.e., in preventing potentially disabling conditions, diseases and injuries from occurring in the first place. The lack of access to health services may result in the occurrence of conditions that may result in disabilities that could have been prevented with timely medical interventions or advice. To illustrate this point, this section looks at how a lack of access to health services in primary disability prevention may result for example in blindness, polio and mental retardation.

To begin with the example of *blindness*, one of its leading causes among children is malnutrition in the form of Vitamin A deficiency. The National Programme for the Prevention of Blindness therefore aims to administer regular doses of Vitamin A to children under five years. However, the National Family Health Service (NFHS 2000) found that on average only three out of ten children aged 12-35 months have received at least one dose of Vitamin A under the National Programme. The Andhra Pradesh rate is below the national average, with only 24.8 per cent of children receiving a dose, and Rajasthan is still worse, in that as few as 17.6 per cent[10] have been administered Vitamin A. Children living in urban areas, children of more educated mothers and children with a high standard of living are more likely than others to receive the dosis (ibid.), which means that the number of poor village children receiving Vitamin A in Rajasthan and Andhra Pradesh is even lower than the rates in the state as a whole. Apart from Vitamin A deficiency, a delay in the detection of eye diseases is a further cause of blindness in children (Rao and Mander 1996). So blindness among children is one example in which access to healthcare can prevent an impairment from occurring through early detection and

Vitamin A supplements. Likewise, the risk of blindness for poor children in rural areas is increased by their lack of access to medical services.

The same is true for *polio*. Access to vaccination just after birth or six weeks after birth can prevent polio. In 1995, the Pulse Polio Immunisation Programme was initiated to eliminate polio in India. However, the NFHS found that while 81.6 per cent of children aged 12-23 months in Andhra Pradesh had received three doses of polio, only 44.6 per cent in Rajasthan had done so, which means that lack of access to the polio campaign leaves every second child vulnerable to this preventable impairment. What is worse, cases of polio infections caused by the vaccine continue to be recorded to this day. Bacquer and Sharma (1997) note that the cold chain required for the vaccine often breaks down between the point of manufacture and the ultimate user-child in rural areas, causing polio cases to emerge as a result of the vaccination.

Another example is *brain damage,* which may result in cerebral palsy or mental retardation. Medical care before, during and after the delivery of a child can reduce the risk of brain damage significantly, especially through the identification of high-risk pregnancies. However, while mothers of 92.7 per cent of children born in Andhra Pradesh received antenatal check-ups in 1999, more than half of the births in Rajasthan in the same year took place without any antenatal care whatsoever. Only 21.5 and 49.8 per cent of deliveries in Rajasthan and Andhra Pradesh respectively took place in health facilities. While in Andhra Pradesh 65.2 per cent of deliveries were assisted by a health professional, this was not the case for the majority of deliveries in Rajasthan. Since a mother's education and standard of living were both found to be negatively correlated with deliveries at home, the risk of brain damage as a result of unprofessional delivery is highest for poor people.

A final example of how lack of access to medical care increases the risk of disability is *mental retardation*. Iodine deficiency is the single most important and preventable cause of mental retardation (NHFS 2000: 274). Iodine deficiency manifestations also include hearing impairment, goitre and cretinism (Park 1998). A study of 1991 found that 42.3 per cent of the iodine deficient population had hearing loss (Roy et al. cited in RCI 2000: 110). One-fifth of pregnant women in India are at considerable risk of giving birth to children who will not reach their optimum physical and mental potential because of maternal iodine deficiency (Vir 1995, quoted in NHFS 2000). Iodine deficiency can be avoided by using salt that has been fortified with iodine and the Government of India has issued regulation[11] fixing a minimum level of iodine in edible salt. The government had launched a National Goitre Control Programme in 1962. In 1986, the programme was re-launched as the National Iodine Deficiency Disorders Control Programme to include not merely goitre but also the other iodine deficiency disorders mental retardation and hearing impairment. The aim was to achieve 100 per cent iodisation of salt by 1992 (RCI 2000). However, over ten years later, this goal has still not been achieved and the risk of disability from iodine deficiency remains high. The majority of households in Andhra Pradesh (i.e., 72.5 per cent) and half of households[12] in Rajasthan use cooking salt with less iodine than is recommended. While lax enforcement, transportation requirements and pricing structures are all explanatory factors for the persistent high usage of non-iodised salt, access to an informed health worker who can warn pregnant women of the potential disabling effects could significantly reduce the risk of mental retardation.

All these examples show how lack of access to health services may result in the occurrence of disabilities that could be prevented with timely medical interventions or advice. Overall it is estimated that as many as 70 per cent of disabilities are preventable (VHAI 1992). Healthcare therefore has a crucial role to play not just in limiting the degree of disability when it has already occurred, e.g., with corrective surgery or physiotherapy, but also in preventing impairments such as blindness, brain damage or polio from happening in the first place. In other words, health services are vital not only in combating the degree or extent of disability, but also its very incidence.

Barriers to Accessing Medical Care

One of the most obvious barriers to medical care for persons with disability in rural areas is *geographical distance* to the next health facility. The Andhra Pradesh survey found that the closest health facility is often located far away from the villages. The nearest hospital to Kanakamamidi and Kethireddipali villages in Rangareddy district was some 40 kilometres away in Hyderabad. Given the poor road conditions and transportation facilities in rural areas, it is difficult to reach medical care facilities for anyone, let alone for persons with disability whose mobility is restricted and who depend on caregivers to take them there.

Even if there is a health centre nearby, disabled people sometimes do not receive treatment there and hence have to travel farther to get the medical care they seek. Villagers said that the hospital in Yenda village in Adilabad district in Andhra Pradesh is always locked up and that they therefore have to travel a further 15 kilometres to the next health facility. People from Bondipalli said that when they go to the primary health centre in Garividi, they are invariably referred to Vizainagram hospital. When they go to Vizainagram hospital, they are refused treatment. Twelve-year-old Narasamma from Timmaraddipalli village went to Madduru hospital twice and was on both occasions sent back home and told to come back later.

Even if a health centre is within reach and the hospital staff receives the patients, *physical barriers* in and around the building often bar access. None of the hospitals that the survey team visited in Andhra Pradesh were barrier-free environments. Many mandal-level hospitals were found not to have any toilets and lacked benches and chairs.

Most hospitals have *no special focus on the disabled*. We have already seen above that specialised doctors are sometimes not even available at the district-level hospitals. The Andhra Pradesh survey found that many district hospitals did not have facilities to treat persons with mental illness. Even medical camps do not take into account the special needs and requirements of disabled people. Insensitivity towards disabled patients on the part of medical staff was a recurring theme in the PRAs. In Bondipalli village disabled people said that hospital staff did not even allow them to sit on the benches while waiting for treatment.

Access to medical care is not only restricted by barriers on the supply side, but also by a *lack of awareness* on the part of disabled people and consequent lack of demand. This prevents them from seeking medical help at several levels. In Andhra Pradesh villagers were found to be unaware of the dates of a medical camp near them, where they could seek medical help. Few people knew of their right to aids and appliances or knew the process of how to obtain them. The survey also found a lack of awareness about the potential of corrective surgery to limit the extent of impairment. This was coupled with rumours that surgeries are of no use, sustained by talk of unsuccessful operations. The surveyors were told that Anjamma and Renuka of Ranga Reddy district as well as Sravanthi of Warangal district had undergone surgical corrections that were unsuccessful. In tribal areas like Paderu mandal disabled people preferred to use herbal medicines, even though the ANM worker advised them to visit a hospital. Five years ago, Appalakonda of Vantlammi village in Paderu sought to heal cataract by putting a leaf extract in his eyes. Today he is blind.

Another barrier to accessing medical care is *economic constraints*. Both the direct costs of treatment as well as the indirect opportunity costs of foregoing wage labour are unaffordable for many. As for the direct costs of treatment, Erb and Harriss-White (2002: 98) estimate that the average annual expenses of disabled adults for clinic visits in rural Tamil Nadu amounted to Rs 1,200 in 1995, which is about a quarter of an average annual household income there. In the three rural villages which the authors studied in Chinglepet district of Tamil Nadu, the cost of surgery ranged from Rs 2,000 to Rs 15,000 (ibid.: 95). Even where medical services are provided free of charge, the patient incurs costs for transport to and from the health facility as well as for the purchase of medication. For many disabled people in rural India this is simply too expensive. The Andhra Pradesh survey came across Subbaya, a fifty-five year old man with leprosy. He told the survey team that even though he had heard that the hospital in Venkatgiri was providing leprosy medication, he was unable to afford the public transport to get to the hospital. Similarly, the survey found that Jogulu from Vantalamamidi village in Visakhapatnam district as well as Himabindu and Parvati of Bondapalli village in Vizainagaram district were unable to undergo eye surgery even though their doctor deemed it necessary, because neither of them was able to afford the direct costs involved. With regard to opportunity costs, the Andhra Pradesh survey found some cases in which the family had taken their disabled children to hospital, but could not follow up with further medical interventions because they could not loose further days of wage income.

Government Policy

In order to understand why medical care is beyond the reach of the majority of disabled people in rural India and how that might be changed, it is important to analyse stated government policy as well as the mechanisms for delivering that policy.

Under the Indian Constitution health is a state subject, which means the provision of medical care and preventive health services is the responsibility of the states. In other words, the state is the ultimate authority responsible for the health services operating in its jurisdiction. The responsibility of the Ministry of Health and Family Welfare at the centre consists mainly of policy making, planning and coordination (Park 1998). Even though most major states have State Planning Commissions, these lack worthwhile health divisions and with excessive centralisation states have become passive associates in planning (Independent Commission on Health 1997). In practice, state funds are almost exclusively spent on curative services (ibid.), while the prevention and control of major diseases are addressed through separate National Health Programmes, sponsored and administered by the Union Government.

The same structure holds for the provision of healthcare services for persons with disabilities. Concerted efforts for the *prevention* of disabilities such as leprosy or blindness are undertaken by the Union Government through certain National Health Programmes run by the Ministry of Health, while those already afflicted with an impairment rely mainly on the mainstream health system for *cure*. In addition, the Ministry for Social Justice and Empowerment contributes to medical *rehabilitation* through its funding of the "complete package" of rehabilitation services provided by the four National Institutes for Disability, of the Rehabilitation Council of India and of voluntary organisations. This section briefly discusses each of these providers of medical care for disabled people.

Apart from the National Programme for the Control of Blindness, the Pulse Polio Programme and the Iodine Deficiency Disorder Programme discussed above, the central government runs two other National Health Programmes directed at the prevention of disability. The National Leprosy Eradication Programme has been in operation since 1955 and was redesigned in 1983 to eliminate leprosy by the year 2000. The strategy adopted is a combination of early detection of cases through trained leprosy workers and multi-drug therapy free of cost to reduce the quantum infection in the population, reduce the sources of infection and break the chain of transmission of disease. While 400,000 new cases were still being detected annually in 1996 (Park 1998: 303), data from March 2003 suggests that fifteen states have achieved the level of leprosy eradication of less than one case per 10,000 population, with six states being close to that level. Only

Bihar, Orissa, Jharkand and Chattisgarh still reported a ratio of five to nine leprosy cases per 10,000 population.[13] The National Mental Health Programme is another health programme with which the Union Government seeks to extent healthcare services to disabled people. Launched during the Seventh Five-Year Plan, the thrust of the programme is to teach PHC physicians and paramedical staff basic knowledge and skills in mental health (Bacquer and Sharma 1997). Other National Health Programmes, such as Child Survival and Safe Motherhood Programme, also have a direct bearing on disability prevention, even though they are not exclusively directed at it. The care of mothers during pregnancy and delivery as well as of newborns can reduce the risk of disability significantly, as was discussed with respect to mental retardation above. Apart from the latter, maternal and newborn care can also reduce the risk of hearing impairment or locomotor disability, for example by avoiding jaundice, septicaemia and head injury in babies, which are major contributory factors to locomotor disability.

The mainstream public health system is usually the first point of call for disabled villagers. And yet the survey findings above showed that PHCs and district hospitals were not equipped to deal with the special requirements of disabled people. Specialist doctors were not available, paramedical staff did not know how to recognise treatable from non-treatable deformities and physiotherapy was not offered. Polio-specialist Dr. Mathew Varghese[14] argues that this is because disability prevention and cure does not figure among the list of treatment priorities formulated by the Planning Commission, passed on to the states by the Union Ministry of Health and then given to the district hospitals as directives. This list determines the kind of health services offered by the hospitals and the staff recruited for the provision thereof. District hospitals are not given a special mandate for the treatment of disabilities and therefore do not even have designated positions for specialists who could provide the health services required by disabled people.

Those institutions which do have a special mandate for the medical rehabilitation of disabled people are not an integral part of the mainstream health system, but are funded by the Ministry for Social Justice and Empowerment. Four national institutes were set up in each major area of disability, i.e., for visual impairment in Dehradun, for locomotor disability in Kolkata, for mental disability in Secunderabad and for hearing impairment in Mumbai. These are responsible for training health professionals, for research into rehabilitation and for producing and disseminating community awareness materials about disability prevention. The Planning Commission (2001) notes that even though these institutes also provide rehabilitation services to disabled people, their reach in rural areas is limited and their outreach initiatives are not enough to cater to the demands of the rural areas where the majority of disabled people in India live. In addition to the national institutes, the Ministry of Social Justice and Empowerment also funds the activities of voluntary organisations in disability prevention and the provision of physiotherapy along with educational and vocational rehabilitation (Erb and Harriss-White 2002). So medical rehabilitation is not an integral part of the mainstream health system, but is carried out by separate organisations as part of a variety of rehabilitation services funded not by the Health Ministry, but the nodal ministry for disability, the Ministry of Social Justice and Empowerment.

Policy Recommendations

The above analysis showed that while medical care has a crucial role to play at all levels of disability prevention, healthcare is beyond the reach of the majority of disabled people in rural India. This is due to a lack of health facilities as well as the poor quality of the existing facilities, combined with a number of other barriers that prevent disabled people from receiving the medical services they require. What is more, the lack of access to timely medical interventions by the rural population in general increases the very incidence of disability, as impairments occur that could have been prevented, e.g., through vaccinations or ante- and post-natal care. The following recommendations are intended to address some of the factors that deny disabled people in rural areas access to health services at each level of disability prevention.

At the primary level the focus needs to be on preventing potentially disabling congenital conditions and diseases through guidance of mothers before and after birth. ANM workers are the main source of health services for many villages in rural India, but the Andhra Pradesh survey found that they generally did not seem to be aware of the importance of pre-natal measures to prevent disability. The same is true for Anganwadi workers. In the three months Anganwadi training only two days are allotted to orientation on symptoms of disability and availability of aids and appliances. Training ANMs and Anganwadi workers in explaining the importance of such preventive measures as Vitamin A supplements, sufficient iodine, polio vaccines and birth attendance to expecting mothers presents a highly effective yet inexpensive opportunity for improving disability prevention. Simple methods of primary disability prevention would need to be incorporated in the general ANM training module the effect would be felt immediately in villages all over the country. It is important that disability prevention is integrated into the general training course of ANMs and not done separately like the RCI training of PHC doctors. Only when disability prevention becomes an integral part of mainstream compulsory training will it be certain that every ANM and Anganwadi worker becomes equipped to prevent and recognise disabilities.

ANMs could be trained not only in preventing impairment, but also in early detection of impairments and subsequent counselling. The earlier an impairment is detected, the greater the chance that corrective measures can minimise its impact. For example, the earlier cerebral palsy is detected, the more improvement can be made in the child's overall development (WHO 1993). Similarly, if an ANM nurse could learn to recognise the early stages of polio in a child when she visits a village, she could immediately advise the family on what exercises with the child's limbs could be done at what stage of the illness to prevent later deformities.[15] Apart from training ANMs and Anganwadi workers, another crucial step in improving primary disability prevention is *better coordination* among the institutions engaged in raising awareness about primary disability prevention among the public and medical staff. The Yavar Jung National Institute for the Hearing Handicapped, for example, regularly holds community awareness workshops about the preventability of hearing impairment (RCI 2002). The other three institutes too prepare and disseminate community awareness material. If the institutes were to coordinate their activities and collaborate to hold workshops about the prevention of not just one but several disabilities, they would be able to achieve broader coverage and greater impact with their limited resources. The same is true for raising awareness about primary disability prevention among medical professionals. It is the mandate of all national institutes to train medical personnel. At the same time, the Rehabilitation Council of India (RCI), established in 1992 as a statutory body for the regulation of the training of rehabilitation professionals, also runs a nationwide orientation programme for PHC medical officers in disability prevention, early identification and referral (RCI 2000). As the Planning Commission (2001) rightly points out, this is not only outside the mandate of the RCI, but also overlaps with the activities of the national institutes. Better coordination between these institutions could enhance the breadth and depth of training in primary disability prevention by eliminating overlap.

At the secondary and tertiary level of disability prevention, improvements should focus on the provision of medical care and aids and appliances in order to enable people to limit the effect of their impairment. As for medical care, *improving the quality of care* is of vital importance in making the most of the existing health system. In the Rajasthan PRAs disabled people demanded supervision of doctors and ANM workers to ensure that they honour their duties. If doctors and nurses attended the primary health centres and hospitals when they are supposed to, the problem of disabled patients having to return home empty handed or having to cross much larger distances to get to the next hospital would be solved. In addition, PRA participants argued that doctors and nurses should be sensitised to the medical needs of disabled people and to the possibilities of limiting the effect of an impairment with corrective surgeries, physiotherapy etc. This is particularly important with congenital deformities. It is only when medical staff know what can be done for disabled people that the existence of a health facility within reach can make a difference in disability prevention. So much could be gained if only the existing health services could work more reliably and be made more sensitive to disabled patients.

Dı Varghese points out that this would require disability prevention and rehabilitation to become an integral part of planning in district hospitals. Not only must disability appear on the treatment priority list, but each district hospital must also be supplied with the number of disabled people in the district as well as the nature of disability. Each district varies in the incidence of particular kinds of disabilities, for example, some districts will have a high incidence of fluorosis-induced disabilities or a particularly high incidence of polio. Lathyrism, for example, a paralysis of the lower limbs resulting from the consumption of Khesari daal, is prevalent only in certain districts of particular states, including Andhra Pradesh, but not Rajasthan. Such locally specific information would help district hospitals to take appropriate measures to ensure that disabled people are catered for in the mainstream medical care system. This would involve both the hiring and training of required specialist such as orthopaedic surgeons but also capacity building of other hospital staff. Even though the district is the administrative unit for the implementation of all health programmes (Independent Commission on Health 1997), district hospitals are not able to respond at the moment to those groups which are at particular risk in their district but not in others, both because they have no mandate for disability treatment and because health planning takes place only at the national level where local specificities are ignored.

Apart from improving the quality of existing services, it is necessary to *extend disability prevention services* to those who live beyond the reach of the present facilities. The most effective and cost-efficient way of doing this is not to build new centres that are expensive to construct, staff and maintain and have a limited catchment area, but to reach out to people with impairments through mobile medical camps. Rao and Mander (1996) advocate camps at the block level or below, staffed by trained disability workers as well as specialists, who could carry out both diagnosis and simple surgery. Such camps could accommodate the demand voiced by disabled people in PRAs in Andhra Pradesh, who said that doctors should undertake detailed examinations of disabled people. Werner (1994) too argues that a detailed examination of each disabled person by specialists is important in identifying potential and for effective interventions. Apart from diagnostic services, these camps could also provide simple corrective surgery for those who need it.

However, Dr Varghese points out that such camps have in the past often suffered from lack of accountability and follow-up, because the operating doctors would be gone after the operation, never to be heard from again, and the doctors posted at the district hospital would have neither the incentive nor the responsibility to follow up each case. He therefore recommends that mobile medical camps only be conducted with the close involvement of the local surgeon, and that the specialists stay back until the local surgeon is confident to handle the cases and their follow-up. In this way medical camps would not only help extend services of disability prevention to disabled people in rural areas who live beyond the reach of existing facilities, but would also help build local capacities by further training surgeons of the district hospitals.

Injury control must become a priority in disability prevention. Injuries are a major cause of disability, but in India have not yet been officially recognised as such. While no official record is maintained by the Indian government of the total number of disabilities resulting from injuries each year, the WHO estimates that there are 12 million injuries in India per year (Alkazi 1992). Approximately, 22 per cent of locomotor disabilities and 3 to 4 per cent of visual as well as speech and hearing disability are due to injuries (NSSO data cited in Bacquer and Sharma 1997: 108). Injuries can occur anywhere and include household injuries, occupational injuries and road accidents. As for occupational injuries, the National Society for Equal Opportunities for the Handicapped in Mumbai estimates that 25,000 industrial workers acquire permanent disability every year due to industrial accidents (ibid.: 108). With 60 per cent of the Indian population working in agriculture, one study (Mohan 1984, cited in Alkazi 1992) estimates that 1 to 2 million agricultural workers are injured every year. Most of these injuries are caused by machine entanglements, especially the chaff-cutter and the thresher. Ten per cent of them are serious and disabling. Household injuries consist mostly of burns and falls. Burns account for 3.3 per cent of amputations in rural areas (Alkazi 1992), and falls may result in all kinds of orthopaedic disabilities or even in skeletal fractures. While there are no official records of the number of people disabled in road accidents, India had the fourth highest accident and death rate in the world in 1986 (ibid.) and one can imagine that for every death there may be many more injuries. Injuries are thus a major cause of disability and must become a priority in disability prevention. Injury control should consist of raising awareness about risk factors at the primary level of prevention, and of early treatment at the secondary level. Sensitisation material, which warns of the risk of common injuries like burns from household fire or poisoning from pesticide, should be developed and distributed to PHCs. Training workshops should be held for ANMs teaching them how to respond in an emergency with early treatment.

Aids and appliances, such as wheelchairs or hearing aids, too can greatly mitigate the extent to which an impairment hinders the ability to perform tasks of daily living. Yet, the survey findings presented above showed that less than 11 per cent of people surveyed in Rajasthan and Andhra Pradesh had received aids and appliances. Recall that in Rajasthan the survey found that 90 per cent of those who received aids and appliances were not using them due to a lack of repair facilities and training as well as unsuitability to local topographic conditions. It is therefore not surprising that in PRAs in Andhra Pradesh disabled people demanded that the government provide aids to more people and that in similar PRAs in Rajasthan disabled people demanded repair and maintenance centres to be set up at the village level.

But this is not enough. The reason why only a few disabled people in rural areas receive aids and appliances, which in any case are not suited to village conditions, is that "we tend to rely on expensive aids and appliances made by urban institutes, many of which are run for profit" (Rao and Mander 1996: 11). These are typically distributed by the state or by charities to few disabled people amidst much fanfare. But given the full magnitude and needs of the disabled, the tangible gains in this are negligible, so that using the scarce funds made available by the government for this amounts to "a blatant misdirection of resources" (ibid.). Rao and Mander recommend instead developing local designs of low-cost aids and appliances using indigenous materials and training local artisans to manufacture these locally. How this can and has been successfully done in India and elsewhere is outlined in detail in Werner (1994), presenting a model of village based rehabilitation workshops run by disabled village workers.

These measures, which improve the supply of medical services and aids at all three levels of disability prevention, need to be complemented with measures tackling barriers to the demand for medical care on behalf of disabled people and their caretakers. The analysis above showed that one of the main factors which prevents disabled people from seeking medical help is a *lack of awareness*. The survey found a lack of awareness both with respect to the importance and

> When Uma and Bas Appalareddy from Bondapalli village in Vizainagaram district in Andhra Pradesh had their first child, everyone in the family was so happy about the birth of a boy that it took them a while before they realised that the boy was not moving in his bed like children usually do. Uma and Bas took the Rs 200 they had saved from wage work and brought their son to the hospital at Garividi. There they were told that their son had polio and would never be able to move and play like other children. Uma and Bas refused to believe this and took a loan to take their child to all the hospitals in Vizainagaram district. Five years later Bas had accumulated debt of Rs 10,000 from the moneylender, but his son was still unable to walk, bathe or eat on his own. The child needs constant care. His grandmother looks after the boy while Uma and Bas work in the fields as wage labourers. This puts the family under further financial strain as the grandmother foregoes the daily income that wage labour would give her.

potential of timely medical interventions to limit the effect of impairment and with respect to knowledge about the available services, e.g., the aids and appliances scheme or dates of medical camps. In the Rajasthan PRAs disabled people suggested that information should be compiled specifically for people with disabilities about existing health schemes and provisions. This information should be disseminated through panchayats, ANM workers and primary health centres. In PRAs in Andhra Pradesh disabled people suggested that workshops be held at the village level to dispel the prevailing myths and misconceptions about disability prevention.

The *benefits of improving disability prevention* are enormous. If Uma and Bas, who spent more than they could afford on medical care (see box above), had been able to receive competent and timely medical advice on what physiotherapy to do with their son in order to avoid polio from paralysing him forever, he may have been able to walk, go to school, participate freely in the community, marry one day and lead an independent adult life in dignity. Not to mention the joy and benefits accruing to his parents and grandmother. Timely medical interventions are vital because they can prevent potentially disabling conditions and diseases from occurring in the first place, can prevent these from developing into impairments when they have occurred and limit the extent and effect of disability. Medical care can thus prevent the severe penalties of disability with respect to education, livelihoods and social exclusion discussed in this book. In so doing it can change the lives not just of those who might otherwise have become disabled, but also of disabled people, their families and their communities forever. What better returns to public investment could the state hope for?

Suvarna from Hoskote in Tumkur district of Karnataka is a mother of two girls. Her husband Sadanand is a bus driver and earns Rs 50 a day. Kavya, their youngest daughter, is four years and Sushmita, the eldest, is six years old. Sushmita has cerebral palsy.

When Suvarna was pregnant with Sushmita, everything went according to plan. It was only when Sushmita was seven months old that her mother noticed a delay in her growth compared to other children of her age. When consulted, the local doctor said that Sushmita would never attain the same maturity as other children. Distraught by this news, Survarna decided to get a second opinion. She took Sushmita to Hiryur, some 150 km away, where she was originally from. After examining her daughter, the doctor there told Suvarna that her child's development could be supported with regular exercises, but that other than that nothing much could be done for her. Refusing to give up, Suvarna next went to see a specialist in Chitradurga, who told her that there is no proper circulation in the brain of her little daughter and therefore no proper coordination in her movements. In one last attempt she took her daughter to Bangalore and had her examined in a hospital by a child specialist. The examination there cost Rs 7,000, paid for entirely by Suvarna's family in Hiryur, because her husband refused to finance his wife's efforts to find a medical solution to their daughter's problems.

For three years Suvarna left her daughter with her mother in Hiryur, as she found it difficult to take care of her daughter herself, especially without the support of her husband. Sushmita could hardly do anything on her own. She always sat in the same place and did not recognize anyone. Now that her daughter lives with her

Contd. on next page...

again in Hoskote, Suvarna says she cannot go anywhere because she cannot leave her alone in the house. As her daughter is getting bigger, it is becoming increasingly difficult to carry her along. When collecting her grains from the local ration shop she has no choice but to leave Sushmita at home, tied to a chair.

One day a physiotherapist from the Narendra Foundation, an NGO, visited Suvarna's house on a survey. He discovered Sushmita alone in a corner.

He spoke to Suvarna and taught her exercises for children with cerebral palsy. He promised her that if done regularly, the exercises would evoke a change in Sushmita. And to Suvarna's surprise he was right: today Sushmita is able to roll over, sit by herself and even recognize people.

She has started to play with her younger sister and with the neighbours' children. Sometimes, when Suvarna is done with her daily household chores, she takes Sushmita to the physiotherapy centre of the Narendra Foundation. Suvarna proudly recalls that a couple of months ago Sushmita smiled at her for the first time. Today she cannot stop smiling.

And yet this great progress is lost on those around Suvarna and Sushmita. "My husband does not take much interest in the child," says Survarna sadly. Her neighbours keep saying that Sushmita should be put into an ashram, since she will never be able to go to the toilet by herself. Suvarna's brother too recommends that Sushmita be given away to a church institution. Suvarna admits that sometimes when she is depressed and can't leave the house because of her daughter she seriously contemplates this option. "But in my heart I know that nobody can take care of Sushmita as well as I do. My love and care for Sushmita have not been wasted. Today she even smiles. Who could abandon such a sweet girl?"

Notes

1. Each government-run primary health centre (PHC) has a group of female health assistants called ANM (Auxiliary Nurse Midwife), who each attend to the basic health needs of a population of 5,000 in the plains and 3,000 in tribal and hilly areas.
2. Cited in Narayan (2003).
3. Data from the Ministry of Health and Family Welfare presented in Figure 3 of Independent Commission on Health (1997).
4. Taken from Table B-13 in "Budget in brief 2003-2004" on www.kerala.gov.in
5. NSSO 1992, cited in Independent Commission on Health (1997), p. 278.
6. Estimate by Erb and Harriss-White (2002) in their study of rural Tamil Nadu.
7. The National Health Policy of 1983, a landmark policy, had strongly called for the creation of an infrastructure for primary healthcare as a means for obtaining the goal of Health for All by the year 2000. This lead to the massive infrastructure expansion under the Sixth and Seventh Plan, creating PHCs and SCs.
8. The WHO (1980) classifies *impairment* as any loss or abnormality of psychological, physiological or anatomical structure or function of the body.
9. The same document defines *disability* as any restriction or lack (resulting from an impairment) of ability to perform an activity in the manner or within the range considered normal for a human being. In other words, disabilities are limitations that a person experiences as a result of an impairment (WHO 1994).
10. NFHS (2000), Table 6.15, p. 215.
11. The Prevention of Food Adulteration Act was amended in 1988 fixing the minimum iodine content of salt. The central government then ordered all states to ban the sale of edible salt that is not iodised. This ban was lifted in 2000.
12. NFHS (2000), Table 7.21, p. 277.

13. Cited in "Leprosy Facts" on www.leprosyindia.org/fac.htm
14. Private communication on 17 May 2004.
15. See WHO (1995) for detailed guidelines on when and how parents can prevent deformities in polio.

3

EDUCATION

Causes and Consequences of Exclusion

Varalakshmi is nine years old and lives in Kanakamamidi village in Rangareddy district of Andhra Pradesh. Both of her legs are affected by polio, as a result of which they fail her completely. She is determined to attend the village school, but just getting there is a daily nightmare. To reach the school she has to crawl on her hands, enduring twenty-five minutes of stones and thorns cutting into her skin, leaving her hands wounded and her clothes torn. As if the humiliation and pain of this were not enough, her classmates shout "Kunti Varalakshmi" (cripple) and ridicule her posture when passing her on the street. And these are good days compared to the rainy season, when the village mud-road becomes flooded and Varalakshmi is unable to get to school at all.

Education Profile

Many disabled children would envy Varalakshmi, for at least she is able to go to school at all. The majority of disabled people in rural India are illiterate. In Andhra Pradesh 62 per cent of disabled survey respondents had never been to school. In Rajasthan 53 per cent of the disabled persons interviewed were illiterate. The NSSO (2003) found for rural India as a whole that 59 per cent of persons with disability above five years were illiterate. The Planning Commission estimates are even more alarming: out of 10.4 million disabled children in the 5 to 14 age group only 60,000 attend special schools, while 65,000 attend normal schools under the IEDC programme discussed later in this chapter. Excluding the disabled children going to normal schools without IEDC benefits who have not been enumerated, these figures would suggest that only 1.2 per cent of disabled children of school-going age are enrolled in school (Planning Commission 2001: 27).

Turning now to the disabled children who have been privileged enough to attend school at all, for many of them this privilege comes to an end with primary school. In Andhra Pradesh half of all disabled students surveyed stop attending school after class five. For 25 per cent of disabled students interviewed in rural Rajasthan education begins and ends in pre-school, which means that they do not even make it to primary school. A further 19 per cent of disabled students drop out after primary school. The NSSO (2003) findings even suggest that as many as 59 per cent of the literate persons with disability have not studied beyond primary school.

The numbers thin out progressively with each higher level of education. Only 8 per cent of all persons with disability surveyed in Andhra Pradesh, 13 per cent of those surveyed in Rajasthan and 10 per cent in rural India as a whole[1] had completed middle school. Even fewer had graduated from secondary school, i.e. 7 per cent in Andhra Pradesh, 9.5 per cent in Rajasthan and 7 per cent in rural India as a whole. Only 6 per cent had attended college in Andhra Pradesh. While the NSSO (2003) found that 1.5 per cent of disabled people in rural India had completed vocational training, only two of the survey respondents in Andhra Pradesh, i.e. 0.02 per cent, had done so. Figure 2.1 below reflects these declining retention rates in rural Rajasthan:

Figure 2.1

Educational Attainment of Disabled People in Rural Rajasthan by Gender (All Ages)

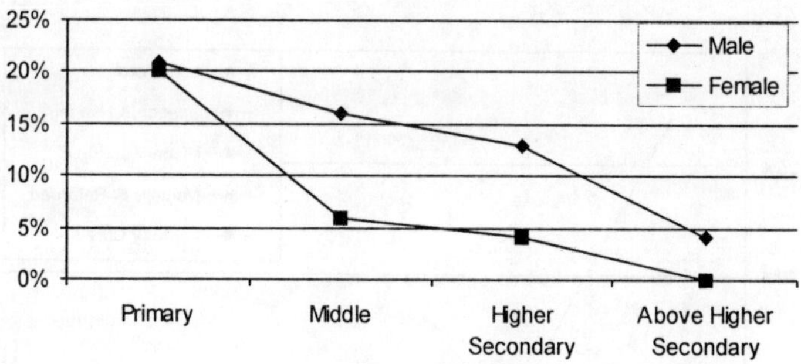

The averages presented above hide the fact that some groups among disabled people fare much worse than others when it comes to education. In particular, educational attainment among the disabled varies by gender, caste and type of disability. Some groups among the disabled face multiple discrimination in addition to their disability, which further weakens their educational status.

Take *gender discrimination.* In both Rajasthan and Andhra Pradesh disabled boys have higher educational attainment than girls at all levels of education as illustrated in Figure 2.1.

Or take *caste discrimination.* The illiteracy rate among dalits and tribals of 66 per cent compares poorly with the 47 per cent among upper castes in Andhra Pradesh. In Rajasthan, the dalit and tribal community have an illiteracy rate of 57 per cent, as opposed to 47 per cent among the upper castes.

Figure 2.2

Education by Type of Disability in Andhra Pradesh

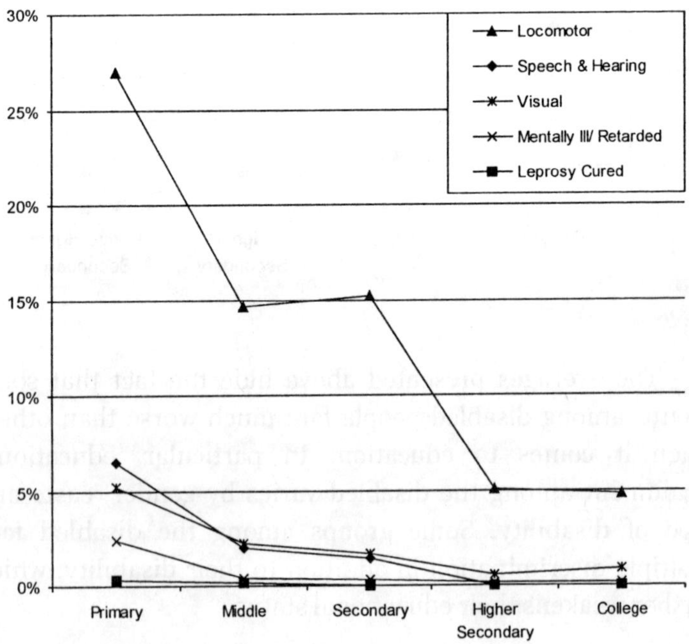

Then there is *discrimination by type of disability*. Figure 2.2 shows that persons with certain types of disability face much more discrimination than others, resulting in differing educational attainments. For example, for 27 per cent of people with locomotor disabilities in Andhra Pradesh education ends after primary school. If you think this a bad ratio, think again: for the speech and hearing impaired, this figure is only 6 per cent, while for the leprosy cured it is zero per cent.

Both the Rajasthan and Andhra Pradesh surveys showed the same pattern of discrimination in education by type of disability: persons with locomotor disability have the highest levels of education, followed in descending order by those with speech and hearing disability, visual impairment, mental illness and retardation as well as leprosy. The latter three groups face the greatest social prejudice and resistance from teachers and fellow students. Visually impaired children have rates of educational attainment that are relatively better, but very poor overall. This should not be so, given that blind children have learning capabilities similar to non-disabled children and can perform well with the help of teaching aids like Braille. Children with speech and hearing impairment have educational attainments similar to the blind. For them it is difficult to grasp anything in the classroom unless a teacher knows sign language. It is not surprising then that relative to all other types of disability, persons with locomotor disabilities have the greatest share of persons acquiring education at all levels. But compared to non-disabled persons, it is hardly an achievement that only 15 per cent of persons with locomotor disabilities have completed middle school, even if this is a better rate of achievement than any of the other types of disability.

Imagine the chances of a mentally retarded dalit girl to overcome the cumulative effect of discrimination on the basis of caste, gender and type of disability to successfully enrol and remain in school.

Barriers to Education

Why is it that the majority of disabled people in rural India are illiterate and that education comes to an early end after primary school even for the privileged minority lucky enough to attend school at all? It is the various geographical, social, physical and attitudinal barriers, which together exclude the majority of disabled villagers from school.

Geographic distance is one such barrier. In Rajasthan, 20 per cent of respondents reported that their village did not have a primary school. For most of the disabled children in those villages getting to a school in another village is simply impossible. To begin with, uneven village roads, full of mud, stones and holes, are anathema to tricycles and crutches, which are designed with an urban topography in mind. A bus stop is often non-existent or very distant. Going by bus is in itself an extremely complicated undertaking for disabled people, given the difficulty of getting onto a bus and the overcrowding inside. In a group exercise in Andhra Pradesh, disabled children pointed out that even when they tried to go by bus, often the bus driver would not stop because they would take a long time to get in. Instead of commuting, non-disabled village children frequently bridge long distances between their home and school by staying in a hostel close to the school. In the group exercise the disabled children said that where such hostels exist, they were typically denied admission.

Distance is not just a geographical concept, but also an emotional one. Even where there is a school in the very same village, the experience of being degraded and embarrassed in public may make the school seem too far to reach in the mind of a disabled child. Varalakshmi is not alone when it comes to derision and harassment of disabled children in public. Without exception, disabled children in all the PRAs carried out in Andhra Pradesh spoke of being humiliated in public including on the way to school. The repeated confrontation with jeering and ridicule evokes a sense of shame and disgrace in disabled children, as they internalise the powerful and dominant social voice of stigma and humiliation.[2] For some the emotional agony of this is such that the distance to school becomes insurmountable.

That education is out of reach for countless disabled children is not just the outcome of geographical or emotional distance. Due to a *lack of parental support* many children never embark on the journey to school, however distant. In 54 per cent of the villages covered in the PRAs in Andhra Pradesh, disabled children said that a lack of support from their parents or caregivers was a significant barrier to their attending school. The high incidence of disability among poor people means that many parents of disabled children lack the wherewithal to send their children to school and often do not know that education is of vital importance in mitigating disability. In addition to the usual gender and caste prejudices that prevent parents from sending even their non-disabled children to school, many disabled children face the further disadvantage that a parent needs to accompany the child to school.

Disabled children of agricultural wage labourers are particularly disadvantaged in this respect, as often even the

> Ekalaxmi is 16. She lives in Vantadapala village in Warangal district of Andhra Pradesh. She was born blind and so has never seen the faces of her parents and seven siblings. She is bright and very social and says she likes looking after her brothers and sisters when her parents are out working in the fields. She sings songs with a beautiful voice. Ekalaxmi has never gone to school. Her father told the survey team "What is the use of getting disabled children educated? It was our destiny to have children with disabilities and now our children have to resign themselves to our fate". Her mother is worried that someone could harm her daughter on the way if she went to school or that Ekalaxmi would fall and get injured. Her sister Mounika, who is partially blind, says that it is in any case no use going, as the teacher does not know Braille. She herself is hardly able to grasp anything in class, as she can hardly see the blackboard. Mounika's classmates make fun of her and constantly ask her why someone "like her" would want to get an education. Ekalaxmi told the surveyors bitterly that she would prefer to be speech and hearing impaired to being blind – at least one would be spared the hurt from hearing the verbal abuse of one's peer group.

mother has to work in the field all day to feed the family and is hence unable to accompany her child to school. In Andhra Pradesh a correlation of family occupation and enrolment of disabled children clearly showed that children of agricultural workers, small farmers and wage labourers have least chance of attending school. Disabled daughters of wage labourers, like Ekalashmi, Vijaya and Nagamma from Vanthadapala village in Andhra Pradesh, are least likely to attend school, since they are usually given the responsibility of taking care of the smaller siblings, the cattle and the household whilst both parents are away working in the fields.

In various PRAs, in both Rajasthan and Andhra Pradesh, parents said that given their children's disabilities, they could see no benefit of investing in their education. Others said they withheld their children from school out of concern about sexual harassment of their disabled daughters or for fear of injury to their deaf or blind children when they cross a road on their way to school.

Even where parents are willing to send their children to school, *physical barriers* in and around the school building make the participation of disabled children difficult. For example, in Gattu village of Andhra Pradesh, the high school has no ramp and is accessible only over high steps, which are difficult to climb with crutches and impossible to surmount with a tricycle. There are no toilet facilities in the school, making it difficult or impossible for disabled children to relieve themselves, as they, unlike their non-disabled classmates, cannot go easily into nearby bushes. In most schools children sit on the floor. In the Rajasthan survey the lack of benches was found to be a huge problem for locomotor disabled children, who have great difficulty sitting down and getting up. Even where there are benches, their design does not suit disabled children, in that the benches are usually high and give no spinal support. In both Andhra Pradesh and Rajasthan, disabled children complained of not being able to use the school's water facility, as the tap was placed too high for them to reach. Some said that waste water stagnating near the tap caused them to fall as they tried to reach the tap on crutches.

Prejudice and lack of training on the part of teachers further obstructs the provision of adequate education for disabled children. In none of the villages surveyed in Andhra Pradesh had the teachers been trained in inclusive education or been sensitised to special needs. In Andhra Pradesh non-disabled children reported that some teachers were calling their disabled classmates by degrading names. Teachers themselves said they did not have the time or capacity to pay special attention to disabled students during class, since they were under pressure to finish the course in time and were already overburdened with too many students. BT Nagar village of Andhra Pradesh is a case in point, where a primary school only had two teachers for 220 students.

In a village in Tipparti mandal of Nalgonda, Andhra Pradesh, a teacher was found to be completely unaware that one of his students was speech and hearing impaired. The student was unable to understand the teaching and subsequently dropped out. Sign language has not been developed in Telugu, the local language in Andhra Pradesh. Similarly, it was found that not a single teacher in any of the villages covered in Rajasthan and Andhra Pradesh knew Braille. With respect to mental retardation, various incidents were reported where teachers overtly barred such children from attending school. Ratna, for example, a girl with mental retardation from the dalit community in Kousalyadevipeta village of Andhra Pradesh, was expelled from school after pinching her classmates. Rajvati, a tribal girl with mild mental retardation from Baran district in Rajasthan, met a similar fate after starting quarrels with her classmates. She has no choice but to stay at home now, helping with housework. Incidents of teachers barring students from attending schools were recorded in as many as 10 per cent of villages covered by the PRAs in Rajasthan.

The surveys suggested that the various barriers to education discussed become greater over time. For example, while disabled students may be able to take humiliation from teachers and classmates initially, their ridicule often becomes unbearable over time. Several locomotor disabled children from Vanthadapala village in Andhra Pradesh said that the humiliation they faced from their peers eventually became so bad point that they could no longer take it and therefore stopped going to school. Similarly, geographic distance as a barrier to education increases with every level of education, in that the higher the level of education the further away the respective school. In Rajasthan, 64 per cent of the villages surveyed did not have a middle school and 88 per cent did not have a secondary school. The need to travel long distances to access higher education deters disabled children in these villages from continuing their schooling. This explains the declining retention rates presented in Figure 2.2 the various barriers to education increase over time and prevent more and more children from going to school.

Contrary to the expectations of many teachers and parents who believe that disabled children cannot and do not want to study, research carried out in ten blocks covered in the Project for Integrated Education of the Disabled Children (PIED) showed that most disabled children performed on par with non-disabled children when the barriers to education are addressed. Disabled children had a much higher retention rate than their non-disabled classmates, on average 91 per cent. Absenteeism was low among disabled children and their achievement levels were at par with the non-disabled students, with orthopeadically handicapped children performing best, followed by the visually and hearing impaired. Children with mental retardation were the only group to perform well below the average of other disabled children. Parental awareness, financial assistance and an improved school climate under the PIED were found to be the most important factors behind the good retention, attendance and achievement rates (cf. Mukhopadhyay and Mani 2002: 102). This shows that when the barriers to education discussed in this section are systematically addressed in a programmatic intervention then a child with disabilities can be just as good a student as any other.

Consequences

When teachers and parents deny a disabled child access to education, they actively prevent the child from developing even the most basic of capabilities, which are crucial to leading a life with confidence and self-respect. Evidence suggests that the critical early years of life are the optimum time for learning basic skills (cf. Alur 2003: 7). The absence of these capabilities condemns disabled children to a state of constant *dependency* on others. Education can reduce this dependency significantly and is therefore of utmost importance to disabled children.

The negation of education is one of the most disabling measures that exist, as it turns a health problem into a permanent *social problem*, laying the foundation for endless future discrimination and humiliation. Without education, disabled children enter the vicious cycle of discrimination based on disability, additional discrimination for being illiterate, lack of ability to speak out against discrimination and so on.

Appanna, who lives in Bondapalli village in Vizainagaram district of Andhra Pradesh, was born without hands. When his mother wanted to enrol him in the local school at the age of five, the teacher refused on the grounds of Appanna's disability. However, his mother did not take no for an answer and after repeated attempts and pleas finally convinced the teacher to accept Appanna as his student. Yet the teacher's scepticism prevailed, as he believed that without hands Appanna would never be able to write and hence also be unable to study properly. To everyone's amazement Appanna taught himself to write with his foot, with a pen delicately balanced between his first and second toe. However, Appanna's education nevertheless came to a premature end in class three, when the teacher struck his name from the school register after Appanna had been bedridden with severe fever for three months.

The denial of education in childhood has life-long *psychological* consequences. The foundations for adulthood are laid during infancy and childhood, so being excluded from something as central to a child's life as school does serious damage to self-worth, confidence and acceptance by oneself and others. The stigma attached to having a disability is thus reinforced very early on in life with the additional stigma of being an outsider from one of the central activities of children. And this is not the only psychological damage caused by denying disabled children access to schools. For children, schools are the main arenas for socialisation among peers. Missing out on this interaction may result in difficulty in relating to others, including peers of the opposite sex, and in alienation from the social environment as these children grow older.

A lack of education narrows livelihood options of even non-disabled children, confining them to low-skill, low-return occupations. "For children with disabilities the risk of *poverty* owing to a lack of education is even higher than for children without disabilities" (Price 2003: 4). Because a lack of education bars disabled children not only from vocational training and employment, but also from participating in a meaningful way in their families and communities, it forever perpetuates their social and economic dependence. This dependence makes uneducated disabled children extremely vulnerable to life-long poverty.

So to deny a disabled child access to education is not just to defy the extraordinary zeal for learning of disabled children like Varalakshmi, who are willing to endure daily humiliation in return for some basic village education. It is not just to refuse Rajvati, Ratni and millions of other children a widely accepted basic human right. It is denying them liberation from the *social and economic dependence* that is the source of the misery in their lives. And it is destroying all hopes for a future free from poverty and a life in dignity and self-respect. Sceptical parents, prejudiced teachers and teasing classmates ought to keep this in mind.

The Government and Education for All

If one were to go by the law, there should not be any disabled children out of school at all. Apart from numerous international declarations that have been ratified by the Indian government,[3] there is also domestic legislation establishing the right to education for all. The Indian Constitution stipulates "the State shall endeavour to provide ... for free and compulsory education for all children" (Directive Principles of State Policy, Article 45). This was made a Fundamental Right in 2002, when the Indian Parliament passed the 86th amendment. A specific reference to the right to education of persons with disability is contained in Article 41, which reads "the State shall, within the limits of its economic capacity and development, make effective provision for the rights to work, to education and to public assistance in cases of unemployment, old age, sickness, disablement and in other cases of undesired want". The Persons with Disabilities Act, 1995 casts a statutory responsibility on the appropriate government and local authorities to ensure that every child with a disability has access to free education in an adequate environment until the age of eighteen (Chapter V, Section 26).

Indeed, in 1992, the universal education of disabled children became declared policy goal. The Programme of Action (PoA), as it became known, was developed following the review of the National Education Policy of 1986 and made a commitment for universal enrolment of disabled children by the end of the Ninth Plan in 2002 in general schools wherever possible, as well as in special schools or in special sections of general schools where needed.

This section takes a look at the main government scheme devised specifically for the education of disabled children in order to understand why universal education among disabled children has remained an elusive goal to this day. The next section then analyses programmes of inclusive education.

The main scheme of the central government for the education of children with disability is the Integrated

Table 2.1

Education Schemes of the Andhra Pradesh Disabled Welfare Department

	Name of scheme	*Eligibility (income below amount in Rs)*	*Category[4] (see notes for key to acronyms)*	*Amount sanctioned*
1	Scholarships for class I to VIII • I to V • VI to VIII	24,000	OH,VH,HH	• Rs 35 per month • Rs 50 per month
2	Scholarships	24,000	OH,VH, HH	
	•Class IX and above IX, X and Intermediate			• Day scholars: 85 per month • Hostellers: 140 per month
	• Degree course or equivalent			• Day scholars: 125 per month • Hostellers: 180 per month
	• Post-graduate/engineering/professional training			• Day scholars: 170 per month • Hostellers: 240 per month
	• Research scholars	12,000	OH, VH	Rs 400 per month
3	Scholarships	12,000	MR	Rs 1,000 per annum
4	Reimbursement of tuition fee to pre-metric students (< class X)	12,000	OH,HH,VH	Rs 25 per month
5	Reimbursement of tuition fee to post-metric students	12,000	OH,HH,VH	Rs 500 per annum
6	Reimbursement of tuition fee to professional courses	12,000	OH,HH,VH	Rs 4,000 per annum

Contd...

Contd...

7	Supply of note books and student stationary like supply of geometry boxes, scales, pencils, erasers, record books, drawing books etc. for hostel students		OH,VH,HH	Rs 150 per annum
8	Note books to hearing impaired students in residential schools		HH	• Class I to V: Rs 70 per month • Class VI to VIII: Rs 100 per month • Class IX and above: Rs 200 per month
9	Braille sheets to visually handicapped students residing in residential schools		VH	Rs 400 per person per annum
10	Braille slates to visually handicapped students residing in residential schools		VH	Rs 150 per person
11	Supply of instruments and books to ITI and Polytechnic students	12,000	OH,VH,HH	• ITI: Rs 80 per month • Polytechnic: 103 to 549 per annum
12	Coaching for competitive, type and shorthand exams	12,000	OH,VH,HH	Rs 18-30 per month depending on exam
13	Readers allowance for students		VH	Rs 25 per month

Education of Disabled Children Scheme (IEDC), launched in 1974. It is sponsored by the Ministry of Human Resource Development and is implemented by the state governments. Among other things, the scheme provides financial assistance for books, transport, hostel charges, escort and reader expenses to disabled students attending common schools. In addition to this scheme, the state governments are meant to disburse scholarships to disabled students attending primary schools without support services. Table 2.1 lists the different schemes offered by the state governments in Andhra Pradesh,[4] while Table 2.2 does so for Rajasthan.

Table 2.2
Education Schemes of Rajasthan Disabled Welfare Department

	Name of scheme	*Eligibility (income below amount in Rs.)*	*Category*[5]	*Amount sanctioned*
1	Scholarships class I to VIII I to IV V to VIII IX to XII above	18,000	OH, VH, HH, MR	Rs 40 per month Rs 50 per month Rs 85-240 per month
2	Hostel Facility	Children of non income-tax payers	All categories	Rs 675 per month

While the mere existence of government support schemes is in itself a laudable fact and distinguishes India from countless other developing countries, a closer look at the present schemes reveals that they suffer from poor design and implementation.

The Rajasthan survey reveals very low rates of scheme coverage, which suggests serious *implementation* problems. Only 12 per cent of disabled school age children received scholarships, only 25 per cent of them received free school books and a mere 0.05 per cent received teaching aids and appliances, even though all of them are entitled to the latter two. Further evidence of implementation problems comes from the Planning Commission (2001), which notes that the efforts made under the IEDC scheme "are almost negligible", in that only 0.6 per cent of disabled children are going to school under the IEDC scheme (p. 27).

Two central problems of implementation are lack of awareness and lack of accessibility. The surveys found *pronounced lack of awareness* among persons with disability of government schemes intended for them. This may explain the low rates of scheme take up to some extent in the sense that people do not apply for schemes they do not know of. But lack of awareness cannot explain away the low take up in its entirety, as awareness rates were invariably found by the surveys to be higher than take up rates, meaning that many more eligible people know about the schemes than get to participate in them. This suggests a lack of accessibility, which is confirmed by the PRA outcomes in Rajasthan. In 70 per cent of villages where the PRA was carried out scholarship schemes were said to be unavailable. Similarly, in 72 per cent of villages teaching aids and appliances were completely unavailable, while free books were not accessible for disabled students in 87 per cent of villages.

A further aspect of implementation problems is the fact that in some states a significant part of the money that the government allocated to education for the disabled is not actually spent in practice, but is returned to the state unused. For example, in Rajasthan, an average of 24 per cent of expenditure allocated to education for disabled children between 1997 and 2001 was not spent. This amounts to Rs 47.3 million of wasted allocated expenditure.[6] Just imagine how many disabled children could have been brought into school with this money in Rajasthan alone.

The bureaucrats who failed to disburse scholarships, free books and appliances to disabled children did not only fail to do their job, but are partly responsible for the perpetuation of the social and economic dependence that continues to haunt these children throughout their lives. This is because, as bureaucrats, they conspired in denying disabled children the thing that could have averted their life-long dependence – education. However, it seems that responsibility for so much misery does not constitute any significant burden on a bureaucrat's conscience, since a constant amount of allocated resources continues to be unspent every year.

The IEDC scheme not only suffers from poor implementation, but also from *inappropriate design*. The scheme is informed by the charity approach to disability, which is in turn based on the medical understanding of disability as a health problem or biological condition. Scholarships and free books are extended by the state to a biologically disadvantaged group of people as measures of charity, and not as a fulfilment of the recipients' right to free education.

Within the medical framework, charity in the form of financial support to disabled students is considered an appropriate policy. However, if one believes the major cause of disability not to be a health problem, but the discriminating behaviour of the environment, then charity is an altogether inadequate response. When disability is construed as a social construct, the sources of disability are to be found not in the disabled person, but in the environment. Policies like scholarships that focus exclusively on the disabled child and ignore the environment are therefore inadequate, as they fail to address the key causes of disability. Scholarships and free aids and appliances are necessary policies, as they help children overcome economic compulsions and mobility problems, but they are not sufficient on their own. The analysis above showed that some of the key barriers to education of disabled children are negative attitude of parents, prejudice of teachers, humiliation from classmates, physical barriers and geographical distance. A policy that is intended to tackle education for disabled children needs to address each of these areas. Possible ways in which this could be done will briefly be explored in the next section.

Special vs Inclusive Education

To meet the challenge of including millions of disabled children in the education system, the policy discourse is increasingly shifting from special education to *inclusive education.*[7] In a country like India, where few resources have to reach millions of disabled people, most of whom live in rural areas, special schools for disabled children are economically unviable and inappropriate. The past record of establishing special schools proves this point. According to Lal (2003), there are a total of 3,000 special schools in India today, concentrated in large cities and therefore inaccessible to most of rural India. No wonder then that most disabled village people interviewed in the Rajasthan survey were not even aware of the existence of special schools. Of the 586,465 villages in the country, a mere 241 have facilities for special schools,[8] and according to Alur (2003) there are entire states which have no special schools at all. In all other villages integrated education is provided "by default" in the village schools, with the result that "integration has been a disaster in most rural areas" (Puri 2003: 10).

Integrated education is not just the most cost-effective means for the education of children with disabilities, but an end in its own right. Inclusion is not just a method, but also a value. As the Kochi declaration of the North-South Dialogue on Inclusive Education Conference in 2003 states, segregation is a violation of human rights, as all children have a right to be included in mainstream local schools (reprinted as Appendix 3 in Alur and Rioux 2004). Inclusion is based on the principle of equal opportunities for all and is valuable in its own right, regardless of its instrumental advantages.

This is not to say that inclusive education is for everyone. Children with severe disabilities may still need special schools (Narayan 1994). But for the majority of children with moderate disabilities inclusive education at the village level is a value as well as a means which can go a very long way indeed in securing education for those currently out of school.

Integrating disabled children in the mainstream education system has been a part of education policy right from the first official attempts of addressing education issues in India (Alur 2003). Even before India attained independence, a report by the British chief educational advisor John Sargent recommended that "provision for the mentally or physically handicapped should form an essential part of a national system of education and should be administered by the Education Department. Wherever possible, handicapped children should not be segregated from normal children" (quoted in Jha 2002). The recommendations of this so-called Sargent Report 1944, a landmark policy document on integration, were echoed in subsequent documents, albeit less strongly. The first educational commission in independent India, known as the Kothari Commission, noted that it is essential that education of handicapped children should be an inseparable part of the general educational system, though it also noted that many handicapped children find it psychologically "disturbing" to be placed in an ordinary school (Alur 2003: 44). The 1968 National Education Policy endorsed the Commission's recommendations by suggesting both the expansion of education facilities for disabled children as well as integrated programmes to enable them to attend ordinary schools. Nearly two decades later, in 1986, the National Policy on Education, which has since been guiding the education system in India (cf. Jha 2002), called for the education of children with mild disabilities in general schools and of those with severe disabilities in special schools. This was echoed more recently in the 1995 Persons with Disabilities Act, Article 26 (b) and (c) of which call on the government to "endeavour to promote the integration of students with disabilities in the normal schools" as well as to promote the establishment of special schools for those in need of them.

However, despite the government's inclusive rhetoric in policy documents, the measures taken in practice to achieve education for all are largely segregative in nature.

Take for example the Union government's most recent education initiative, which contains specific measures to implement inclusive education. The Sarva Shiksha Abhiyan, programme, launched in June 2003, aims to provide quality education for *all* children between six and fourteen years by the year 2010. Under this programme, one disability "resource teacher" is to be assigned in each block, whose role is to advise the village school teachers and also plan individual education programmes for all disabled children in the block. In addition, a resource centre for disabled children is to be established in each block. Finally, at the district and state levels, separate planners should be appointed to implement and monitor inclusive education. Contrary to the policy aim of integrating disabled children in the mainstream education system, these specific measures in fact promote segregation. The appointment of special teachers, who organise individual interventions for disabled children in their block, cannot be called an inclusive policy. Similarly, the new posts of separate planners for inclusive education at the district and state levels constitute an artificial segregation of accountability, creating the false impression that disability "is being dealt with" and hence not the responsibility of the gender, pedagogy or other planners (Commonwealth Education Fund 2003).

Alur (2003) observed a similar discrepancy between "policy and its implementation, not in keeping with the declared policy of Education for All" (p. 215) in the government's Integrated Child Development Scheme (ICDS). The scheme provides basic health care and pre-school education for poor children between 0 and 6 years. While the declared policy intent is that the scheme is for "*all* needy children" (ibid.), Alur found in her research in Dharavi, a large slum in Mumbai, that children with disabilities are excluded from government pre-school nurseries. "While policy makers may be discussing integration at the top level, practice at the bottom level reveals a lack of authentic movement towards placing the disabled child into regular classrooms" (p. 97).

One reason for continued divisive policy measures despite inclusive policy rhetoric may be that education of children with disabilities has still not become an inseparable part of the administration of the general education system, as the Sargent Report had originally called for. In other words, while the IEDC scheme is administered by the Education Department, the education of disabled children in special schools still remains the responsibility of the Ministry for Social Justice and Empowerment, which fulfils this role by making grants to NGOs for the provision of special education. Alur (2003) argues that this is an indication of the lack of the government's commitment to the integration of disabled children in the mainstream system. Until and unless responsibility for the education of all disabled children: whether in special or in normal schools rests with the main policy making body in the field of education, their true and meaningful integration in the general education system would seem unlikely.

We have seen thus far that while inclusive education is the only viable and appropriate form of education for most children with disabilities in India, there is a discrepancy between the government's inclusive policy rhetoric and its policy implementation, which is largely segregative in nature. The problem with this is that by definition segregative policy measures cannot bring about successful inclusion. Nor can policies which are inclusive in letter but segregate in actual fact. In order to make village schools that are inclusive "by default" into schools that are inclusive "by design", the concept of special education needs to be turned on its head: instead of changing disabled children to fit into the "normal" society, it is the "normal" schools that have to change so that disabled children can participate in them. This requires far more than simply relocating special education "from segregation to regular schools and calling it inclusion" (Jha 2002: 129). Inclusion efforts must not go on in isolation and consequently be perceived as an external and isolated process for the support of students with disabilities, as it is currently the case, but be an integral part of general school reform and restructuring (ibid.).

Inclusion is a reform process that requires the participation of all stakeholders in a school, be it students, teachers, headmasters, parents, members of the Village Education Council, architects, builders or administrators. It cannot be administered top down by a block-level special teacher or a state-level planner, as envisaged in the Sarva Shiksha Abhiyan. A school only becomes and remains inclusive if those who are involved in it on a daily basis make every effort to facilitate the participation and acceptance of children with disabilities. Only with the support and commitment of the school staff and community at the grassroots can the limited available resources be used creatively to turn each and every village school in the country into an accessible and inclusive learning environment that can live up to its default role of providing education for all.

The potential benefits of inclusive education are enormous: not only could disabled village children finally attain education, but village society as a whole could become more inclusive. This is because inclusive education is capable of breaking the vicious cycle of segregation in childhood leading to segregation in adult life. Baquer and Sharma (1997) argue that the school is the ideal place to start the difficult process of creating a society where being different is accepted, respected and valued. What is more, education tends to improve for everyone when children with disabilities are included in the classroom: the majority of the general teachers who underwent training in inclusion under the PIED programme indicated that they were becoming better teachers by teaching disabled children (quoted in Jha 2002: 101). Mukhopadhyay and Mani (2002: 100) too note that "integration of disabled children has actually reinforced better educational practices in the general school system".

Policy Recommendations

The principal aim of any education policy for disabled children must be to remove barriers to education and *create an enabling environment*. This is the policy priority of disabled persons in rural Rajasthan and Andhra Pradesh, as reflected in the surveys conducted in the two states. All of the recommendations made by the disabled persons interviewed were invariably directed at their physical and social environment. This section briefly looks at the various suggestions and their policy implications.

A first step to create an enabling environment quite literally is the *removal of physical barriers* in and around the school building. Disabled children in both Rajasthan and Andhra Pradesh said that ramps, proper benches and toilets are minimum requirements.

In both states disabled people further suggested that *workshops* be held in their villages to *raise awareness* about the vital importance of education to disabled children. While the primary target group for such workshops are parents and carers, non-disabled school children, teachers and members of the Village Education Council should also participate and be sensitised to disabled children's right to education and need thereof.

Disabled people in both states expressed the necessity to make inclusive education methods an integral component of any *teacher training*. Since the Rajasthan survey found that there are at least five disabled children of school age in any village, and since special schools are out of reach, every teacher will have disabled students at one point or the other in his or her career. Only if teachers are sensitised to special needs in their training will they be able to recognise them in their classrooms and know how to respond to them. For example, in Andhra Pradesh, respondents said that teachers should learn basic sign language, so as to improve communication with speech and hearing impaired students. Moreover, Puri (2003) argues that teachers need to be trained in dealing with all disabilities, and not just specialise in a single disability, as is most often the case. Already, programmes exist for training teachers in inclusive education. The Rehabilitation Council of India (RCI) runs a bridge course for training special teachers who are already working in the field of disability but do not have special training or qualification. The RCI has also initiated distance teacher training courses with the Madhya Pradesh Bhoj Open University in Bhopal and the Indira Gandhi National Open University (Planning Commission 2001). In the mainstream university system too, schemes for teacher training in disability education are offered by the University Grants Commission and in some states special education has been included in pre-service and bachelor courses (Jha 2002). Under the District Primary Education Programme (DPEP) for the universalisation of elementary education, states are incorporating integrated education in their general in-service teacher training. It is the implementation of the latter which is most important, for this is the only way in which to ensure that future generations of teachers will all be equipped with skills to successfully implement inclusive education in their classrooms.

Since some key barriers to education are social barriers, an enabling environment can only be created through direct *involvement of the local community*, as for example in the village awareness workshops. Only a change in the attitude of teachers and parents in the village itself can bring about inclusion. In this process, disabled persons have a crucial role to play. They know their needs and preferences best and an

Anand is the son of a poor farmer in Chandrai village of Nagaur district in Rajasthan. At the age of eight an illness rendered him blind. At a nearby eye camp a doctor diagnosed Anand's blindness as incurable, but encouraged his father to send him to a school for the blind in Ajmer, a town some 150 km away from his village. It took the doctor several months of continued persuasion before Anand's father agreed. Anand very much valued his privilege to attend school and laboriously studied until graduating from the College in Ajmer with excellent marks. His dream was to be a teacher and so he sat and passed the B.Ed. Entrance Test. However, he was refused admission to the College on the grounds that it had no adequate provisions for blind students. Anand appealed to the High Court and won his case. Today Anand is the teacher he wanted to be, and says he is very content to be able to make a meaningful contribution to the community in this role.

environment can only ever become truly enabling if their voices are heard and acted upon. In both Rajasthan and Andhra Pradesh survey respondents suggested that persons with disabilities be assigned key positions in implementing policy.

When contemplating the difficulties involved in bringing about inclusive education that deserves the name, we should not forget Anand's story. His story illustrates the crucial role education plays in harnessing the enormous dormant potential of disabled children. Access to education enabled Anand to realise his dream of becoming a teacher. Imagine the potential contribution that millions of disabled children, who unlike Anand remain illiterate, could make if only they

When Kannagi was born, there were no celebrations. She was the second daughter born to poor parents. And she was blind. Her father Ganesh, a mouse catcher in the village of Thiruchirapalli, Tamil Nadu, thought she was a curse to the family. He often came back home drunk and beat up Kannagi's mother, Vijayalakshmi. Most of her early childhood was spent alone in a dark room She barely heard any voices and rarely moved from her bed. "She ate very little and her body hardly grew in the first seven years. Her limbs were stiff and there was no coordination between them," recalls her mother. Her visual impairment stunted her overall physical growth to the extent that the villagers declared her a 'dwarf'. A dwarf was not welcome anywhere. And Kannagi's family in any case did not think she needed to go out and breathe fresh air or soak herself in the sun. What difference would that make, they shrugged, she can't see anyway.

After eight years of such existence, a group of young women from a local NGO called the Society for Education Village and Improvement (SEVAI) came to Kannagi's home and told her parents that she too could learn and grow and even go to school. Initially Kannagi's parents were skeptical and hesitant. In their village disabled children were usually kept inside the house, confined to loneliness and shame. But the young women insisted that Kannagi be given a chance. They had heard rumours in the village that Kannagi could recite lengthy Tamil poems having listened to them only once.

In the beginning, the SEVAI special educators visited Kannagi's home to play with her and teach her the basic skills of grasping and holding objects. They also took her to their Resource Centre, where Kannagi learned about her country, state, village and rivers with

Contd. on next page...

several local materials like bindis, sea shells, wool, shirt buttons, bangles and charts.

Gradually, Kannagi came out of her confinement and started mingling with other children and the neighbours. The NGO gave her a walker, which greatly helped her mobility. Kannagi's mother observed that "Initially, my daughter did not have an appetite. But after she started communicating with others, she started eating regularly. Now she not only eats by herself, but manages to wash her hands and rinse her mouth after food. Her laughter echoes in the entire village".

Once Kannagi gained confidence, she was very eager to go to school. Her father Ganesh, decided to support her when he realized the enormous progress in his daughter. He gave up drinking and even tried to learn Braille to teach his daughter. The villagers noticed how a very transformed Ganesh would frequently teach Kannagi patiently. In 2001 Kannagi boarded the bus to school for the first time and joined class one. She soon became a fan: "I love school. I tell my friends a lot of jokes. I don't want to miss school for a single day" she says.

were allowed to attend school. This contribution would make a difference not just to themselves, but also to their parents, their siblings, their own children, to other disabled persons and to their communities at large. Denying disabled children access to education is a tremendous waste of potential. Even a country as large as India cannot afford to forget millions of its children.

Notes

1. The latter according to NSSO (2003).
2. On the latter, see Ghai (2003), p. 59.
3. For a brief review of international conventions on the right to education see Brohier (2002).
4. Key to acronyms: HH = Hearing Handicapped (includes speech handicapped), MI = Mentally Ill, MR = Mentally Retarded, OH = Orthopaedically Handicapped, VH = Visually Handicapped. Information as listed in "Status of Implementation of Persons with Disabilities (Equal Opportunities, Protection of Rights and Full Participation) Act, 1995 in Andhra Pradesh" presented by the Disabled Welfare Department, Government of Andhra Pradesh at the National Conference of the Disability State Commissioners in Bangalore on 22 June 2001.
5. Key to acronyms: HH = Hearing Handicapped (includes speech handicapped), MI = Mentally Ill, MR = Mentally Retarded, OH = Orthopaedically Handicapped, VH = Visually Handicapped. Compiled from the following documents: Rajasthan Social Welfare Department (2003). "Annual Report 2002-03". Jaipur: Government of Rajasthan; Rajasthan Social Welfare Department (2002). "Guidelines for Persons with Disabilities". Jaipur: Government of Rajasthan. (Hindi booklet); Rajasthan Social Welfare Department (2002). "Welfare Activities for Persons with Disabilities". Jaipur: Government of Rajasthan.
6. This was calculated on the basis of budget data presented in Table 27 on page 42 in a budget report prepared by the Rajasthan Budget Analysis Centre for the ActionAid Rajasthan Regional Office in 2003.
7. The term "inclusive education" originated in disability studies and is therefore most often associated with the inclusion of persons with disabilities. However, "inclusion" in India should more adequately encompass the many other groups excluded from education, such as children of sex workers, street children,

children with HIV/AIDS, tribal children, displaced children etc. For the purposes of this book, inclusion is used in the narrow sense of disabled children only.

8. Data Source: Sixth All India Educational Survey Report cited in Puri (2003).

4

LIVELIHOODS

Poverty and Policy

"Employment is vital for one's living", argues Datrange (2002: 36). It is a means to fill empty stomachs and may give an individual self-esteem and a sense of purpose. But in rural India *employment is beyond the reach of the majority of disabled people*. The Rajasthan survey, for example, revealed that 62 per cent of disabled villagers over 18 years are altogether without work. In Andhra Pradesh 51 per cent of the disabled people interviewed in the survey were unemployed. The NSSO (2003) data paints an even bleaker picture. It reports that only 26 per cent of disabled people in rural India are employed, which means that 74 per cent of them were not engaged in any economic activity. When this is disaggregated by gender it emerges that 63 per cent of men and an incredible 89 per cent of women were economically inactive.

Among the disabled, some people are more likely to be without work than others. Figure 3.1 presents unemployment rates among the disabled persons over 18 years surveyed in

Figure 3.1
Unemployment Rates by Types of Disability in Rajasthan

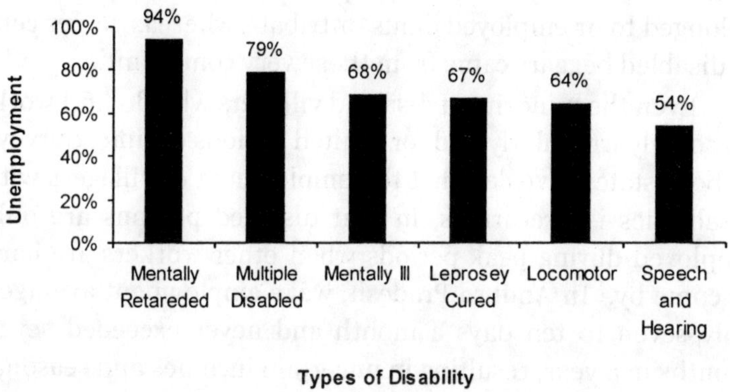

Rajasthan. It indicates that unemployment rates vary by *type of disability*, the pattern of which could be called a "hierarchy of disadvantage" with respect to employment. Persons with mental retardation are the most disadvantaged group, in that as many as 94 per cent of them do not earn a living in Rajasthan. The situation of people with multiple disabilities is equally bad. Visually impaired people are much more fortunate – they have the highest work participation rates among disabled people, followed by the speech and hearing disabled and persons with locomotor disabilities. The NSSO (2003) too shows that among the disabled, persons with speech and hearing, locomotor or visual impairment have the highest employment rates in India, while persons with mental retardation are the most disadvantaged. The NSSO found that only 6 per cent of persons with mental retardation were employed in rural India, which confirms the survey's finding in rural Rajasthan as shown in Figure 3.1.

Apart from the type of disability, *caste* also matters when it comes to employment. Only 23 per cent of the petty businesses run by disabled people in rural Andhra Pradesh belonged to or employed dalits or tribals, whereas 76 per cent of disabled beggars came from those very communities.

Even the minority of disabled villagers who do find work, do so only irregularly and for limited periods of time. Surveys in both states revealed that the employment of villagers with disabilities is precarious, in that disabled persons are only employed during peak periods when other workers are hard to come by.[1] In Andhra Pradesh, wage employment averaged only seven to ten days a month and never exceeded seven months in a year, resulting in uncertain incomes and seasonal shortfalls.

Occupational Profile

In rural Andhra Pradesh and Rajasthan, the majority of those disabled people lucky enough to find work at all do so in *agriculture* (see Figure 3.2). In Andhra Pradesh 85 per cent of disabled people working in agriculture do not cultivate their own land, but work as wage labourers.

Apart from agriculture, disabled people work in their own or someone else's petty business, selling vegetables, milk or cloth. Some do skilled work like carpentry or mechanics. Contrary to the perception that *begging* is the principal occupation of disabled persons, only 2 per cent in Andhra Pradesh and 4 per cent in Rajasthan reported begging as their main occupation. The Rajasthan survey found the largest proportion of beggars among people with mental illness.

In Rajasthan, the survey also found disabled teachers and government employees, albeit very few in number. This occupational profile of disabled people closely mirrors that of

Figure 3.2

Occupations of Disabled Persons above 15 Years in Andhra Pradesh

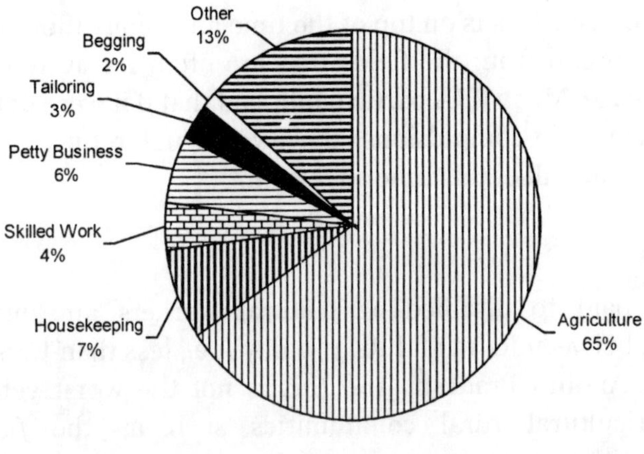

rural India in general, where livelihood options are dominated by agriculture, where work is predominantly physical in nature, and where intellectual opportunities are few and far between.

The physical exigencies of agricultural work challenge and pain even the strongest of able-bodied persons and are totally inappropriate for most disabled people. In the PRAs conducted in rural Andhra Pradesh, survey respondents recalled the agony of having to bend over for hours and lift heavy weights, when even handling crutches presented a big challenge to them. They said the normal nine to ten hour working day of an agricultural wage labourer is insufferable, as they are not allowed to take even a short break from the hard physical work in between. Their employers are completely insensitive to their needs and co-workers make things worse by mocking them. Disabled workers generally work longer hours than their able-bodied colleagues, either because their employer will only hire them if they "make up" for their disability by working longer, or because they themselves find that they need more time to complete the assigned task. This is on top of the time and agony they spent getting to and from the fields that are often far away from their village. Many PRA participants said that if it were not for their economic compulsions, they would not return to the field and face all of this time and again.

Incomes

Wages paid to disabled agricultural workers are pitiful, varying between Rs 15 and Rs 35 a day (i.e., less than US$ 1 a day) in Andhra Pradesh. And this is not the worst yet: in non-agricultural rural communities such as the *fisher communities* on the east coast of Andhra Pradesh, disabled people are confined to low-return jobs like rope making or drying and knitting fisher nets, which earn them as little as Rs 100 to Rs 300 a month (i.e., less than US$ 6.60 a month). To survive on such pitiful wages is very difficult indeed. Disabled people in *tribal areas* face similar hardship, as workers in these communities are paid per amount of forest produce they gather. The undulating terrain in tribal areas presents a big physical challenge to the disabled, whose consequent inability to gather any significant quantities of fire wood or herbs directly results in economic hardship.

These wage rates are far below the statutory minimum wage of Rs 61 a day for unskilled labour in rural Andhra Pradesh. They are also far below the wages received by able-bodied workers for the same job. For example, in Narsimhulupeta village of Warangal district in Andhra Pradesh, the survey found discrimination in wage rates for speech and hearing impaired agricultural wage labourers. The

Rajasthan survey found that employers generally bargained for lower wages for disabled workers, pointing out their disability and employing them only if they were ready to accept very low wages. Erb and Harriss-White (2002) find in their study of three villages in Chinglepet district of Tamil Nadu that discrimination in wage rates for the same work on account of perceived differences in physical strength is a socially acceptable way for landowners to reduce labour cost (cf. p. 43). The experience of wage discrimination of disabled people in rural India is in line with the experience of disabled workers in developed countries: Barnes and Mercer (2003) cite four studies from the US, UK, Australia and Canada, which show that disabled employees earn considerably less than their non-disabled counterparts in these countries.

Although only 42 disabled persons provided reliable information on their monthly incomes in Rajasthan, the pattern that emerges even from this very small sample as represented in Figure 3.3 is a harrowing illustration of the

Figure 3.3
Income of Disabled Persons in Rajasthan (Rs per month)

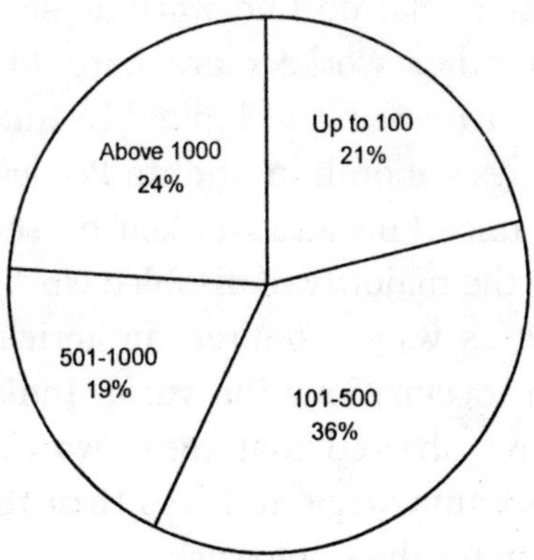

extent to which disability causes poverty. Recall that 62 per cent of the disabled people of working age surveyed in Rajasthan are without work and therefore totally dependent on their family for survival. As for the disabled people lucky enough to find work, 21 per cent of those who reported their incomes earn less than Rs 100 a month, which means they have to manage with three to four rupees a day! Altogether, the majority (57 per cent) earn less than Rs 500 a month, which amounts to Rs 16 (US$ 0.37) a day. This is a far cry from the World Bank poverty line of US$ 1 a day.

Disability and Poverty

It is worth pausing here to appreciate the *employment scenario* with respect to disability in Indian villages in its entirety. We have seen thus far that the majority of disabled people in rural India are unemployed, with some groups among the disabled being almost entirely excluded from the labour market. Recall for example that unemployment rates are as high as 94 per cent among persons with mental retardation in Rajasthan. We have further seen that the lucky few disabled villagers who do find work do so only during peak periods when other workers are hard to come by. Their employment is irregular and limited in time, averaging only seven to ten days a month in Andhra Pradesh. Their incomes are therefore uncertain and marked by seasonal shortfalls. What is more, the majority of disabled workers in the villages surveyed work as wage labourers in agriculture, one of the lowest return occupations in rural India. The evidence presented above showed that these workers earn incomes below the minimum wage and less than their non-disabled co-workers earn for the same work.

In light of this scenario it is not hard to imagine that *disability is a cause of poverty*. The dynamics are as follows: When disabled villagers are unable to find sufficiently paid regular work as described above, they become dependent on their family for survival. This presents a burden on the family income in at least two ways. Firstly, the family needs to cover not only the usual costs of living such as food and clothing of the disabled person, but also the additional costs resulting from the disability such as medical treatment and aids and appliances. Secondly, the family looses out on labour contributions of that individual to the household income. Erb and Harriss-White (2002) find in their study of villages in Tamil Nadu that in the case of a man, the loss of earnings through disability plunges an agricultural labouring household directly into debt, whereas when the income contribution of a woman is lost, the average income of such a household declines by one-third. Where a family member is required to be with the disabled person during the day as carer, the household income is further reduced by the earnings foregone by the carer.

As a result of these dynamics, households with disabled members are disproportionately among the poor. Harriss-White (1999), for example, found that a higher proportion of households with self-reported disabled members in three villages in Tamil Nadu were below the income poverty line than households without disabled members. Households with disabled members also had lower assets, smaller operational landholdings and higher levels of debt than those without.

Apart from livelihoods, there are also other, non-economic dimensions of disability which contribute to the material impoverishment of persons with disability and their families. These include the denial of access to free education, healthcare and rehabilitation services, as well as exclusion from community activities discussed in the other chapters of this book. These dimensions are separate yet not independent of the livelihoods dimension, as they aggravate the economic impoverishment of disabled villagers. Lack of free healthcare, for example, has a direct impact on economic status as it necessitates spending on private healthcare. Social exclusion from community activities may reduce the chance of finding employment

In addition to being a cause of poverty, *disability is also a consequence of poverty*. The leading causes of impairment are malnutrition, diseases and accidents (cf. UN figures cited in DFID 2000: 3). The poorest households are most susceptible to these causes of disability, as the conditions of poverty increase their exposure to disabling circumstances. "Poor households do not have adequate food, basic sanitation and access to preventive healthcare. They live in lower quality housing and work in more dangerous occupations" (Elwan 1999: 34). In this way, the circumstances of poverty increase the risk of disability caused by malnutrition, diseases and accidents. Evidence for this comes from a survey of Bombay conducted by the Spastics Society of India in 1986, which found that the incidence of disability amongst children was highest in the slums of the city (cited in Alur 2003).

The two processes of disability being both a cause and a consequence of poverty interlink to form a "vicious cycle" of poverty and disability wherein one exacerbates the other. Disability adds to the risk of poverty and the conditions of poverty in turn increase the risk of becoming disabled. It is because of this close association of disability with poverty that disability must be considered and dealt with as a core development issue, and not, as is presently the case, "be considered a specialist issue separate from mainstream development issues" (Yeo 2001: 8).

Consequences of Low Insecure Wages and Unemployment

It is almost impossible for urban Indians or international readers to fully appreciate the hardship entailed in coping with only Rs 16 a day, who easily spend this amount on a small bag of potato chips. In rural India, disabled people and their families routinely live with *hunger*. While their neighbours may migrate during the off-season to avoid starvation, for many disabled people even this basic coping mechanism is not an option, given the lack of demand for disabled workers and restricted mobility.

But hunger is not poverty's only toll. *Dignity* too suffers beyond imagination when purses remain empty. Having to depend on the goodwill of others for even the most basic of material needs, not being able to afford any clothing other than rags and not being able to provide for the well-being of one's own children would damage the self-esteem of anyone. But, for disabled people, the indignity of economic hardship comes on top of the humiliation they face for being different. Rahmad Bano, a forty year old woman from Nagaur district in Rajasthan, has a spinal injury that confines her to beg for a living. She says that as a result of her poverty her relatives shun her house and never visit. In cases like her's it is difficult to say what is harder: coping with the disability, coping with the ensuing poverty or coping with the indignity originating from either.

Apart from hunger and indignity, poverty also causes *voicelessness*. When half of the disabled people surveyed in rural India have no means of earning a living whatsoever and the majority of the other half earn less than Rs 16 a day,

Durgamma is a twenty-eight year old woman from Annavaram village in Visakhapatnam district of Andhra Pradesh. She gradually started loosing her eyesight from the age of ten, and was totally blind by the time she reached puberty. In despair, her father and mother took her to all medical centres in her and the neighbouring district. Despite spending more money than they could afford on medication and treatment, doctors finally declared after seven years of treatment that nothing could be done to restore Durgamma's eyesight. By this time her father had accumulated debt of Rs 22,000 for the medical expenses and was struggling to meet even the increasing demands in interest rates from the moneylender, let alone pay back the principal amount. When her father died in the year 2001, Durgamma and her mother were left alone in the house with no means of income. Her two brothers and elder sister had married long ago, and Durgamma was the only child for whom it had turned out to be impossible to find a match, given her blindness. So, when her father died, Durgamma and her mother had to find a way to support themselves and so took up making thread from coconut fibre. Even though they work until late at night each day, they are never able to avail more than Rs 50 to 100 a week for their produce. They are dependent on the subsidised rations of basic staple food allotted under the BPL* card scheme. However, these are rarely enough and for ten days a month Durgamma and her mother go hungry.

* BPL stands for "Below Poverty Line". BPL cards are issued by the government to families with an income below the poverty line. The card entitles them to buy basic commodities at subsidised rates at outlets of the Public Distribution System.

survival is the only thing on anyone's mind. With everyone struggling to secure the next meal, who is able to stand up and raise their voice to demand a livelihood, equal wages and proper treatment? Who will have the resources, time and courage to point out that disabled people in rural India live in extreme poverty and indignity? Poverty silences people and their silence in turn perpetuates their poverty.

Barriers to Employment

Why are millions of disabled people without work in India? Surely not all of them can be unemployable. Even a person with multiple disabilities has countless abilities for which he or she could be gainfully employed. So to construe unemployment among the disabled purely as a supply problem is overly simplistic. Rather, unemployment seems to be the outcome of both demand and supply deficiencies.

With respect to labour supply, the *low levels of education* described in the previous chapter may act as a constraint to recruiting disabled people into skill-based occupations and thus confine them to physical work like agricultural labour, which is least suitable to them. While it is true that in rural areas higher education does not necessarily translate into better livelihood options, it is also true that a lack of basic education bars people from entering occupations outside the physical realm of agricultural work. Without being functionally literate or numerate, village people cannot become petty business owners. For disabled people, who in any case face multiple layers of discrimination, education is even more important in order to obtain gainful non-agricultural employment.

A further supply constraint is *physical accessibility*, which frequently prevents disabled people to pursue a given career even if they are qualified. Getting to the workplace entails the same problems that disabled children face on their way to school, as described in the previous chapter. At the workplace, stairs, inaccessible toilets and narrow doors make life difficult to impossible for the disabled employee. "Don't drink anything before you go to work" is the advice Murthy (2003: 1) gets from a friend, who says she may not be able to find an accessible rest room there. "Help, help" yells a senior colleague of hers, when his wheelchair gets stuck in a doorway. Physical barriers like these prevent Murthy's friends from taking up the jobs they are qualified for. One of her friends, paralysed by a spinal cord injury, says, "I can't think of taking up projects outside the house". For a physically challenged person, access to places means "access to their life" (ibid.).

As for the demand for disabled workers, one key constraint is the widespread perception that disabled employees are not efficient or productive. Arora (2001) argues that it is this impression, compounded by a lack of awareness of the potential of persons with disabilities, which keeps public and private employers in India from taking on disabled workers. However, Barnes et al (1999: 113) cite studies in the UK and the US, which show that disabled workers generally have better sickness records and are often more productive than their able-bodied peers. One can easily make out jobs in which disabled people would be "better-abled" in that they would perform better than their non-disabled peers. Hearing impaired persons, for example, would be able to concentrate better in high-noise environments such as workshops or computer data entry in large offices. Similarly, persons with visual impairment "can do rather better than normal persons in dark room situations" (Pandey and Advani 1995: 102). So employing disabled persons can make very good business sense indeed. The idea that disabled people are unproductive is therefore a *social barrier* to employment, in that it is the attitude of the social environment, not the actual productivity, which excludes disabled people from work.

This reluctance on the part of employers to hire disabled staff is compounded in the private sector by the *lack of a disability policy* in all industrial chambers. As Javed Abidi, Director of the National Centre for the Promotion of Employment for Disabled People[2], points out, none of the major four industrial chambers[3] has a policy on employment of disabled people. He explains that while the Confederation of Indian Industries (CII) added disability to its social agenda after much lobbying in 2003, it has not moved anywhere close to translating this into policy. If even the big four industrial chambers in India are unwilling to articulate a policy on the employment of disabled people, how are medium and small enterprises in rural areas supposed to be sensitive to disabled people and recognise the abilities they could be employed for?

Government Schemes

Unlike many other developing countries, the Government of India has given employment of disabled people special consideration. However, the implementation of its schemes has been deficient.

In 1977, the Government of India *reserved* 3 per cent of vacancies in identified jobs in government and the public sector in groups C and D[4] for persons with locomotor, visual or speech and hearing disabilities. The 1995 Persons with Disabilities Act extended this reservation to groups A and B. Mentally disabled persons are excluded from reservations, even though the National Institute for the Mentally

Handicapped has identified a long list of jobs that can be done by persons with mental retardation.

While the reservation of jobs for disabled people is a very welcome government initiative, the implementation of this provision has been found wanting. A study of 20 public sector companies showed that only 0.54 per cent of employees were disabled (NCPEDP 1999). The backlog of placements needs to be fulfilled immediately. Similarly, government jobs in the A and B categories have not been filled with disabled candidates, even though the reservation in these groups has now been in existence for eight years. In the year 2001-02 five persons with disabilities reportedly cleared the three rounds of the civil services examination on merit but were denied entry into the Indian Administrative Service on grounds of their disability.[5] What is more, the government has to date not even produced the required list of identified jobs for these categories. It has also failed to revise the existing list of identified jobs in the C and D groups, even though the Supreme Court ordered it to do so in 1999. Pandey and Advani (1995) argue that the existing list is outdated and inappropriate, as many jobs that are known to be suitable for people with different types of disability have not been included. Furthermore, the spread of technology and the availability of improved aids and appliances make reservation against certain pre-identified posts counter-productive, as more and more jobs can be done by disabled people with the help of new technology. Pandey and Advani therefore advocate abolishing the identification of posts altogether.

As for the private sector, Section 41 of the Persons with Disabilities Act, 1995 stipulates that the government is to provide *incentives to companies* to ensure that at least 5 per cent of their workforce is composed of persons with disabilities. Regrettably, even ten years later this well-intentioned law has still not been translated into policy.

The central government is sponsoring a scheme called "Employment of the Handicapped" through 40 *Special Employment Exchanges* as well as 41 special cells for disabled people in regular Employment Exchanges. The objective of the scheme is to bring persons with disabilities into gainful employment. The Planning Commission (2001) judges the scheme to be a failure, given that in 1999 only 1.06 per cent of unemployed disabled people registered with these Exchanges were actually placed in jobs (p. 22). Furthermore, the vast majority of those placed are persons with locomotor disabilities (cf. Baquer and Sharma 1997: 129) and the scheme has done little to nothing for the millions of people in India who have other types of disability.

In 1997, the National Handicapped Finance and Development Corporation (NHFDC) was incorporated, as a not-for-profit company wholly owned by the government. It was endowed with Rs 4 billion to extend loans to disabled people for pursuing higher education, upgrading technical and entrepreneurial skills and setting up small enterprises. The NHFDC's micro-finance scheme, for example, provides loans of Rs 10,000 to disabled persons for income-generating activities. While the potential of this organisation is enormous, there are serious problems in realising it. The Planning Commission (2001) notes that the reach of the NHFDC is very limited, particularly in rural areas and that there is considerable delay in the processing of applications for loans.

The Government of India is also providing *vocational training* to disabled people through 17 Vocational Rehabilitation Centres (VRCs) across the country. These centres are located in 16 state capitals and are therefore beyond reach for

> Arockiadass was struck by polio as a little child and is severely crippled. The loss of control over his limbs was not to be the only one in his life. He soon lost his mother too, who like him had suffered from polio. His aged grandmother struggled to bring him up on the little she earned as a coolie. He completed ninth grade with great difficulty. After many years of marginalized existence, Arockiadass finally found employment in a small electrical shop as an errand boy. The shop owner paid him a mere Rs 8 a day, arguing that this wage was more than the due of a disabled person. This attitude incited Arockiadass to prove to the world that disabled people can match and even outperform their able-bodied colleagues and therefore deserve equal pay. He worked with a fervour and enthusiasm that even the shop owner could not fail to notice and after three years finally obtained a pay rise to Rs 25 a day. This sum would seem too small to write home about for many, but it meant the world to Arockiadass, who says his pay rise was a moral victory for all disabled people. Encouraged by the success of his personal struggle, he went on to struggle for and with other disabled people for better livelihoods. He uses his connections with the civil bureaucracy to get permission for other disabled people to open phone booths or petty shops and thus earn a livelihood.

the majority of disabled people who live in rural areas. During the Sixth Plan period the government sought to address this problem by adding 11 Rural Rehabilitation Extension Centres (Baquer and Sharma 1997). However, these were concentrated in only five of India's 720 districts.[6] It is not surprising therefore that the Planning Commission found that "the available programmes cater largely to the needs of the organised sector in urban areas" and that rural areas are completely neglected in the provision of vocational training for disabled people (Planning Commission 2001: 28). In addition to the VRCs specifically intended for persons with disability, the government also reserves 3 per cent of vacancies in its craftsmen training programme for disabled people (ibid.), which are carried out by the government-run Industrial Training Institutes (ITIs). Like the VRCs, these institutes are concentrated in cities and therefore inaccessible for the majority of disabled people in rural India.

Apart from policies to foster employment amongst disabled people, there are also a small number of government schemes, such as pensions and unemployment allowance for disabled persons, or material support such as financial assistance with transport costs. Table 3.1[7] shows an example of such schemes in Andhra Pradesh, while Table 3.2 shows this for Rajasthan.

Table 3.1

Economic Welfare Schemes of the Andhra Pradesh Disabled Welfare Department

	Name of scheme	*Eligibility (income below amount in Rs)*	*Category*	*Amount sanctioned*
1	Unemployment allowance		All categories except MR	Rs 75 per month
2	Economic rehabilitation	11,000	All categories except MR	Rs 3,000
3	Disabled pensions		All categories	Rs 75 per month
4	Transport allowance		OH	Rs 50 per month
5	Petrol/diesel subsidy	24,000	OH, VH, HH	15 liters per month permissible (2 horse power and below) 25 liters per month permissible (more the 2 horse power)

Table 3.2

Economic Welfare Schemes of Rajasthan Disabled Welfare Department[8]

	Name of scheme	*Eligibility (income below amount in Rs)*	*Category*	*Amount sanctioned*
1	Unemployment allowance		All categories except MR	Rs 200 per month (max. for three years)
2	Economic rehabilitation	12,000	All categories except MR	Rs 2,000
3	Disabled pensions	2,400 (age 8 years and above)	All categories	Rs 200 per month
4	Train concession	Severely disabled	OH, VI, MI, MR	Attendant free and 50% concession in the fare
5	Bus concession		OH, HH VI MI, MR	60% discount on express bus 100% discount in express bus PWDs free and 50% discount to attendant (two seats reserved for PWDs in the bus)

Policy Recommendations

Apart from implementing existing government schemes better, a concerted effort needs to be made to bring disabled people into jobs that are most suitable to them. The physically disabled, for example, need to be employed in occupations that are less physically excruciating than agricultural labour, the mainfest inappropriateness of which has been illustrated above. Bringing disabled people into viable alternative occupations involves interventions both on the supply and the demand side. Primary education, vocational training and cheap credit on the supply side are just as important as advocacy in private sector firms or the creation of cooperatives on the demand side. Moreover, bringing disabled people into suitable vocations will involve mobilising many different agents of change, including the government, NGOs and business. This section takes a look at some of the things that can be done to end the extensive unemployment among disabled people.

Perhaps the most straightforward way of bringing disabled people into occupations that are suitable to them is to *promote self-employment*. When setting up their own enterprises, disabled people automatically choose an area in which they can best use their abilities and are able to compete with others. Neufeldt and Albright (1998), for example, argue that self-employment is a viable alternative to wage employment for disabled people and has the potential to end reliance on familial assistance. But this outcome does not arise automatically. Instead, the barriers to business start-ups have to be removed and entrepreneurial initiatives have to be facilitated and nurtured. Cheap credit is one such barrier. Private and public banks alike should extend the concessions they make in interest rates to women, religious minorities, scheduled castes and tribes to disabled people as well. At present, banks are not only not giving loans at concessional rates to disabled entrepreneurs, but many of them are not giving any loans at all. They typically consider disabled persons a bad credit risk. But Singh (1995) argues that running a business is such an uphill struggle for a disabled person that those who decide to go ahead with it despite of this will invariably put in much more effort and time than any non-disabled person would. This is why banks have in fact "a greater chance of recovering their loans from disabled persons" (ibid.: 52).

Rasal Kanwar from village Khari Khurd in Jodhpur district of Rajasthan was born blind. She did not go to school and was married when she was eight years old. Her husband was a well-known person and commanded respect from all castes in the village. He was regarded as being visionary and courageous for having taken the bold decision to marry a blind woman. Rasal gave birth to a girl and five boys. Her husband died when the eldest child was only twelve. Widowed with six children to feed, Rasal kept the family alive by working their field with some help from her children, taking up any opportunity to earn extra income on the side. She sent all her children to school and one of her sons got a job in the Forest Department. The villagers were stunned and impressed when they realised that Rasal, a blind widow, did not resign to begging for a livelihood after the death of her husband and that she could achieve as much and more than others despite her disability. Rasal does not have a disability certificate and has never claimed welfare assistance on account of her disability.

Not everyone has the talent, education or motivation to start a business, so other employment generating measures have to be developed in addition to the promotion of self-employment. Datrange (2002) points out that *sheltered workshops* and *cooperatives* have a high potential for mass employment of disabled persons. These could comprise *home worker schemes* for those with severe restrictions on mobility. Given growing trends of outsourcing in the wake of globalisation, there are an increasing number of work opportunities that could be harnessed by disabled people working from their homes, even if they live in villages. Since sheltered workshops, cooperatives and home worker schemes require collective action, it is important that NGOs and the government take a lead in facilitating the establishment of such organisations.

Many of the jobs that disabled persons can do are in the private sector. When left to its own devices, the private sector does not tend to employ significant numbers of disabled people. A study of the top 100 industries in India (NCPEDP 1999) revealed that 20 out of the 70 respondent companies did not employ any disabled people at all, whereas overall disabled people only constituted 0.4 per cent of employees. When the big corporates, who have the financial resources and the job volume to employ disabled people, choose not to do so, one can hardly expect the small and medium enterprises in semi-urban and rural areas to do so.

The experience of Titan Watches Ltd in Tamil Nadu (Deenadayalan 1990) illustrates why most companies are reluctant to recruit disabled people. Many Titan line managers perceived the employment of disabled people as an act of charity and frequently regard them as obstacles to reaching their performance targets. Only when some of the disabled workers outperformed their able-bodied colleagues did some Titan line supervisors accept that the recruitment of disabled persons was based on individual capabilities that in turn are related to performance.

In order to rectify the present situation in which companies of any size are reluctant to recruit disabled employees, even though many disabled people have abilities with which they can match or exceed the performance of their non-disabled colleagues, the government needs to develop a viable *incentives policy*. China, for example, has a policy under which companies in which disabled workers comprise at least 50% of the workforce are exempt from all taxes. In 1987, as many as 70 per cent of the disabled, who were capable of working, had been employed in China (Pandey and Advani 1995). Clearly, a smart incentives policy can go a long way in bringing disabled people into private sector employment.

Equally important to an incentives policy is *advocacy* by disabled groups with firms of all sizes. These groups need to raise awareness among private sector employers about the work that can be done by people with various types of disability. They need to disseminate best practices and lessons learned. Only if employers understand that hiring disabled people in suitable jobs can make good business sense, will they even consider employing significant numbers of disabled workers.

None of these efforts to augment the demand for disabled workers will have any effect without corresponding education and training efforts on the supply side. First and foremost, *literacy* rates among the rural disabled population have to be improved significantly so that they become eligible for non-physical jobs. In addition to this, *vocational training schemes* need to be initiated, which are accessible for disabled people in rural India and which adequately prepare them for suitable jobs.

The existing training schemes run by the government and NGOs are both insufficient and inappropriate. We have seen above that the government's provision of vocational training to disabled people through the VRCs and ITIs is confined to a few urban centres and therefore inaccessible for most disabled people in rural areas. Even though there are an estimated 142 voluntary organisations[9] that provide vocational training to disabled people, NGOs have not fared much better than the government in their training efforts in that the training they provide is inappropriate. An NCPEDP study found that the vast majority of NGO training programmes are focused on low-return artisan work like embroidery and weaving (NCPEDP 1998). These professions are outdated and unsuited to the majority of disabled people. Weaving, for example, puts unnecessary strain on the remaining sight of a partially blind person. More importantly training in artisan skills is inappropriate because it confines disabled people to low-return employment. This is reflected in the dismal salaries obtained by disabled people who found a job through an NGO placement: the NCPEDP study found that more than 41 per cent of them were placed in jobs earning them less than Rs 1,000 a month, far below the minimum wage (ibid.: 32). Vocational training efforts by NGOs need to be reoriented towards jobs that are suitable to disabled people and have the potential to lift them out of poverty. The provision of vocational training that is both accessible and appropriate is of vital importance if disabled people are to stand a chance in the labour market.

The most important thing in translating the goodwill of the government, NGOs and the private sector into solutions that suit disabled people is to *involve persons with disability in decision-making* during the planning and implementation phase. Ministries and NGOs alike need to hire disabled people to design and implement the interventions intended for them. Only then will policies and programmes finally meet the real needs of disabled people. The failure to recruit disabled people into government A and B group jobs means that they are conspicuously absent from decision-making and planning in the ministries. What is even more shocking is that NGOs, which champion the cause of the disabled, are similarly discriminating. A study of disability NGOs by NCPEDP (1998: 14) revealed that less than 22 per cent of the members of disability NGOs' executive bodies in India are persons with disabilities, of which only 3.3 per cent are disabled women. No wonder then that the government and NGO schemes and programmes designed for the vocational rehabilitation of disabled people discussed above fail to meet the needs of their intended beneficiaries. Change has to begin here if anywhere.

Marakka from Kunihalli village in Karnataka is 26 years and mentally challenged. She sits silently next to her mother Anjamma, as she tells their story. Anjamma's mother, i.e., Marakka's grandmother, had been mentally ill and died young. "Someone in the village had evil intentions towards our family, that's why my mother was mentally ill," says Anjamma. After her mother's death, Anjamma's marriage was arranged, to her own uncle, her mother's brother. The couple has two sons and two daughters. For a long time Anjamma did not realise that one of her daughters, Marakka, was also mentally challenged. Even in the village school nobody recognised the disability initially. The teachers tried to teach Marakka how to write, but she could only scribble incoherently. She never spoke in class and was always alone. After three years the schoolmaster declared that Marakka would never learn and struck her name off the register. It was when Anjamma had to continue to comb Marakka's hair, dress and bathe her even at a later age that she realised that Marakka was not like other children.

Contd. on next page...

Being the eldest of two daughters, Anjamma inherited three acres of land from her father when he died. She and her husband grow groundnuts on their land, but for the past three years the rainfall has been very poor and they have not been able to harvest much. In fact they are lucky if they even get enough seeds to sow the next crop. In addition, Anjamma's husband rears two cows, while she works as a wage labourer on other people's fields.

Sometimes Marakka worked along with her mother in the fields, but was never paid. The employers say that she can't work on her own and so does not deserve pay. It is true that she cannot work alone. But when her mother shows her what to do and how to do it, Marakka can do most things. In their own field, for example, she helps to pluck the groundnuts or takes their cows to graze.

The refusal of the employers to pay her worries Marakka's parents. "As long as we live we will take care of her, but what will happen to her when we are no more?" asks Anjamma. Marriage is out of the question for them. If she had a regular income someone or the other would feed her for money, says Anjamma. And so they are trying to get a disability certificate, which is necessary for securing a pension from the government.

Notes

1. Hyde (1996, 1998), who found evidence of this phenomenon in the UK where disabled workers are generally excluded from the workforce except when labour is in short supply or when the

economy is "booming", has used the Marxist concept of a "reserve army of labour" in this context (discussed in Barnes and Mercer 2003: 47).

2. Private communication on 11 December 2003.
3. These are Confederation of Indian Industries (CII), Federation of Indian Chambers of Commerce and Industry (FICCI), Associated Chambers of Commerce and Industry (ASSOCHAM) and Punjab, Haryana and Delhi Chamber of Commerce (PHD).
4. Government jobs are divided into four categories, with group A being the most senior and highest salaried one.
5. *Hindustan Times*, 13 December 2003, 'Disabled Qualifiers denied IAS Berths'.
6. Census 2001 data from http://www.censusindia.net/data/chapter2.pdf
7. *Key to acronyms*: HH = Hearing Handicapped (includes speech handicapped), MI = Mentally Ill, MR = Mentally Retarded, OH = Orthopaedically Handicapped, VH = Visually Handicapped. As listed in "Status of Implementation of Persons with Disabilities (Equal Opportunities, Protection of Rights and Full Participation) Act, 1995 in Andhra Pradesh" presented by the Disabled Welfare Department, Government of Andhra Pradesh at the National Conference of the Disability State Commissioners in Bangalore on 22 June 2001.
8. *Key to acronyms*: HH = Hearing Handicapped (includes speech handicapped), MI = Mentally Ill, MR = Mentally Retarded, OH = Orthopaedically Handicapped, VH = Visually Handicapped. Compiled from the following documents: Rajasthan Social Welfare Department (2003). "Annual Report 2002-03". Jaipur: Government of Rajasthan; Rajasthan Social Welfare Department (2002). "Guidelines for Persons with Disabilities". Jaipur: Government of Rajasthan. (Hindi booklet); Rajasthan Social Welfare Department (2002). "Welfare Activities for Persons with Disabilities". Jaipur: Government of Rajasthan.
9. Figure cited in Baquer and Sharma (1997: 131).

5

SOCIAL LIFE
Beliefs and Practices

> *"Indian society, although 'inclusive' in accepting and valuing diversity in so many ways, has a social construct of disability which is negative, discriminatory and exclusionary"* (Alur 2001: 290).

According to the social model of disability, it is not the individual medical condition but society which disables people with impairments. It is the way in which others react to disabled people that determines whether an impairment will result in the exclusion of disabled people from mainstream activities. Coleridge (1993) argues that if able-bodied people did not react with horror, fear, anxiety, distaste, hostility or patronising behaviour towards disabled people, then there would be no problem. It is discrimination and prejudice that create the sense of being disabled. Seen from this perspective, social exclusion is the most important aspect of disability.

The previous chapters already discussed the social exclusion of disabled people in the fields of education, the labour market and medical care. The survey findings in Andhra Pradesh and Rajasthan presented therein demonstrated for example that disabled students are ridiculed and called by degrading names by school teachers and fellow students. Recall that disabled children in all the PRAs carried out in Andhra Pradesh spoke of having been humiliated in public. The survey also provided ample evidence of social exclusion in the workplace, where disabled people were either not hired or otherwise mocked by their non-disabled colleagues and employers. The livelihoods chapter also illustrated the indignity associated with economic dependence as a result of being excluded from the labour market and the social sanctions of being both disabled and destitute. The chapter on medical care provided evidence of lack of access to basic healthcare facilities and insensitivity towards disabled patients on the part of medical staff. So even up to this point we have seen that social exclusion of disabled people takes place across a number of fields and prevents them from engaging in mainstream society.

Having covered social exclusion in education, the labour market and medical care, this chapter looks specifically at exclusion of people with disabilities from social life. It does so by focusing on attitudes and behaviour towards disabled people in the family, in marriage and in the wider community.

Participation in Social Life

One way in which to assess to what extent disabled people are integrated in society is to look at their participation in social, religious and political functions. The Rajasthan survey reveals that *participation in social functions* varies a great deal by type of disability. While 72 per cent of people with locomotor disability get invited to social functions, only 35 per cent of mentally retarded persons get asked. Along with people with mental illness and multiple disabilities, those with mental retardation are the most socially excluded, in that they have the highest proportion of people who have not attended a single social function in one year. The same pattern emerges for *participation in religious functions*.

In a study of disabled people in 41 villages in Tamil Nadu, Novemoney and Raj (2003: 17) find that "quite a large number of disabled people felt that the community did not accept them and hence they isolated themselves from social activities". The majority of the disabled people in that study, who had never participated in community activities, said that this was due to their disability, while 19 per cent said it was on account of an inferiority complex.

42 per cent of the disabled respondents in the Rajasthan survey say they do not have a single friend. The majority (72 per cent) of those who report having one or more friends say that all of their friends are disabled as well. This means that the majority of disabled people in rural Rajasthan are unable to make non-disabled friends.

The picture that emerges with respect to *political functions* is similarly grim. 90 per cent of disabled people surveyed in Rajasthan have not attended a single gram sabha[1] meeting in the past year. In only two out of 55 villages surveyed had a disabled person been elected to a panchayat.[2] Because it is so rare for people with disabilities to be accepted in community leadership roles, their participation in decisions affecting their lives at the village level is negligible.

Attitudes

What bars so many disabled people from participating in social, religious and political functions? Seeley (2001: 2) argues that "the greatest obstacle to participation and equity is the prevalence of deep-rooted negative attitudes on the part of non-disabled people in the family and community".

Social integration begins and ends in the family. It is at home that a child first acquires an attitude towards himself and the world. "If the parents think that his disability is an overwhelming calamity which makes life worthless, the child will also think likewise; if they are bitter against an unjust fate, he will think so too" (Bhatt 1985: 109). Of course every family is different, and so are their reactions to disability. The parental response to disability found in the Andhra Pradesh survey varied between *overprotection and complete neglect*.

Chadam Maro, a tribal born blind from Adilababad district of Andhra Pradesh, experienced nothing but neglect from his family. He was six when his father died. His mother told him that since he was blind, it was not her business to provide him food free of cost. She sent him to work in the fields. There he fell into a well and was injured badly. Chadam's mother told him that he may as well have died and refused to pay for any medical treatment. Now she simply ignores his presence in the house.

Jangamala, on the other hand, has been overprotected by her parents since birth. As the only child of a Dalit family from Nizamabad district, she told the surveyors that she was given all the love and affection any child could hope for. In her childhood, her parents spent all their savings on medical treatment for her multiple disabilities. Later, when she had a high-risk pregnancy, her father took on debt to have her treated in the district hospital. Her parents are so concerned about her that they never let Jangamala go anywhere on her own. As a result, she never went to school. Werner (1994) argues that overprotection prevents disabled children like Jangamala from developing skills and learning to care for themselves. Because they are not allowed to go anywhere on their own and participate freely in the life of the community, everyone assumes that they cannot and should not. And the fact that the community thinks that disabled children cannot engage in everyday social life means that these children experience "unrelenting socialisation to low expectations or an 'abnormal' life-style" (Barnes and Mercer 2003: 62). In this way, the low expectations that a community has of children with disabilities are just as crippling and oppressive as hostility and rejection (Naidu 2004).

Apart from overprotection and complete neglect, the Andhra Pradesh survey also found cases of *absolute denial.* For example, the father of Ekkama, a disabled girl from Warrangal district, tells everyone who cares to listen that he only has normal children. Similarly, the parents of Ramlamma of Visakhaparnam district hide the fact that her daughter suffers from mental illness. They did not tell her husband of her condition before the wedding, who immediately sought to divorce her when he found out thereafter.

While every family is different in their attitude towards disabled children, their behaviour is influenced by certain common external factors. In a study of 46 villages in West Bengal, Pal et al (2002) found that negative societal attitudes towards disability and social support from *family and friends* affect how well parents adapt to having a child with epilepsy. The severity of the disability was also an important predictor of parental adjustment.

Ramdas and Mishra (1987) argue that prevailing notions of disability have greatly influenced the degree and nature of social prejudice towards the disabled over time. In *Indian mythology and history*, disabled people have been depicted as "cruel and spiteful" (Bhambani 2003: 78). The two most popular Hindu epics, the Mahabharata and Ramayana, project a negative image of disability. In the former epic, king Dhritrashtra is deprived of the throne because he is visually impaired. In both epics disability is associated with evil, in that the central turn comes with the intervention of Shakuni, an orthopaedically impaired man, and Manthra, a dwarf woman who are both presented as evil (Ghai 2003: 47).

But it is not just ancient religious myths that conceptualise disability in negative terms. Today's popular culture too is dominated by negative images of disabled people. *Hindi cinema* plays a central role in this respect. Given that 50 per cent of the population are illiterate, the visual images of Hindi cinema have a powerful and lasting impact on its viewers. Bhambani (2003) shows that in the majority of films disability is either ridiculed and made fun of or pitied and patronised. The abilities of disabled women are never or rarely projected. Nor are disabled people portrayed as making any contribution to the family income. Thus, a powerful media creates and reinforces the stigma of disability and lays the foundation for prejudice and discrimination.

In rural areas many non-scientific explanations of disability exist, which are the cause of much stigmatisation and discrimination. Prominent among these is the view that the birth of a disabled child is a *bad omen*. Suramma from a village in Vizainagaram district of Andhra Pradesh is a case in point. When her youngest son was born, he had

Mahalaxmi is a 28-year-old woman from a tribal village in Visakhapatnam district of Andhra Pradesh. She was born mentally retarded. Her parents and brother have all passed away. The village street used to be her home and she eats whatever food passers-by give to her. Due to the stigma attached to mental retardation, the villagers would never consider marrying their sons to Mahalaxmi, or even take her into their house. It was therefore a big shock to everyone when it suddenly became evident that Mahalaxmi was five months pregnant. A local NGO convened a meeting in the village and cajoled the villagers into taking responsibility for the situation. A visit to the hospital revealed that Mahalaxmi was malnourished, anaemic and did not have enough blood to deliver a child. The villagers came forward to construct a small hut for her, the NGO agreed to pay for the hospital fees and a food stall owner made a commitment to feed both Mahalaxmi and her baby.

such tiny hands that the midwife ran out of the house screaming the child was a bad omen. Suramma's friends and relatives, who used to visit her regularly, also began to shun her house.

Ramdas and Mishra (1987) found in their study of a district in West Bengal that the most prevalent view of disability there was to see the impairment as an outcome of the parents' *karma*. Based on the Hindu belief of reincarnation, the birth of a disabled child is seen as a punishment for sins committed in a previous life. The Andhra Pradesh survey too found many cases in which the disabled people themselves and the community believed both congenital and acquired disabilities to be caused by karma.

Alur (2001) argues that seeing a disabled child as one's *karma* entails viewing the child and the disability as one's personal tragedy and therefore as one's individual responsibility. In this view society and the state have no role to play. Disability exists only outside the public domain and is something to be hidden behind the four walls of one's private sphere. "Disability has long been perceived as an individual problem, therefore resulting in the indifference of the society and the state" (Mohit 2000).

The extent of social exclusion is often dependent on the type of disability. People with mental illness face the worst degree of discrimination and exclusion from the community. Seetamma from Gattu village in Chitoor district of Andhra Pradesh has experienced many a manifestation of her community's disdain for people they consider mad. Most days Seetamma can be found at the village bus stop, singing songs and dancing to them. With passers-by calling her mad or averting their eyes, it is hard to imagine that as a child Seetamma had many friends with whom she climbed trees and played hide and seek in the very same village. It was the hardship and grief Seetamma experienced on her husband's death that took a toll on her mental well-being and changed her life forever. Loosing her beloved husband and becoming widowed with three young children and a mountain of unpaid medical bills traumatised her irrevocably. Instead of helping Seetamma at this critical moment when she was so clearly in need of care and affection, the villagers asserted that she must be possessed by some evil spirit and ordered an exorcist to drive the spirit away by conducting spiritual mantra on her.

When this failed to cure her, some villagers began to overtly steal things from Seetamma's house, saying that as a mad person she no longer had a right to her belongings. The community considers her a total outcast. Her brother in law forcibly took away the 5 acres of land that her late husband had inherited. The experience of daily humiliation has left Seetamma bitter and desolate. "Only when I dance can I forget the injustice of it all", she says.

Marriage: Data and Trends

Marriage is a crucial aspect of social life, especially in India, where the institution of marriage is all-important. Table 5.1 presents the questionnaire data concerning marriage collected in the Rajasthan survey. To understand how this compares with marriage patterns of the population as a whole, Table 5.2 presents marriage data obtained in the 1991 census for rural Rajasthan.

Table 5.1

Proportion of Married Disabled Persons in Rural Rajasthan

Age group	*Male*			*Female*		
	Total	*Married*	*Per cent married*	*Total*	*Married*	*Per cent married*
Up to 13	127	3	2	80	0	0
14-18	88	7	8	50	14	28
19-25	117	36	31	60	47	78
Above 25	300	234	78	168	157	93
Total	632	280	44	358	218	61

Table 5.2
Proportion of Married Persons in Total Population of Rural Rajasthan[3]

Age group	Male			Female		
	Total	*Married*	*Per cent married*	*Total*	*Married*	*Per cent married*
Up to 14	311,554	3,420	1	258,580	5,670	2
15-19	75,960	14,120	19	48,840	28,000	57
20-24	58,230	35,950	62	51,312	49,902	97
Above 25	582,284	46,5731	80	489,080	465,090	95
Total	1,028,028	519,221	51	847,812	548,662	65

Keeping in mind that the two tables are not strictly comparable, given that the disability data emanates from a sample survey whereas the data for the population as a whole is census data and was collected 12 years prior to this, one can nevertheless make out the following indicative trends:

Firstly, the *proportion of disabled persons who are married*[4] *is smaller* than the proportion of married persons in the population as a whole. This is true for both men and women and for all age groups. For example, while 62 per cent of men between the age of 19 and 25 years are married in rural Rajasthan, only 32 per cent of disabled men of that age are married. However, the difference between the proportion of married people among the disabled and the total population narrows down to only 2 per cent for the age group above 25 years.

This brings us to the second point. Disabled people in rural Rajasthan tend to *get married later in life* than the population at large, as suggested by the fact that in the younger age groups few disabled people get married compared to the population as a whole, whereas there is hardly any difference (2 per cent) above 25 years. In other words, people with disabilities "catch up" with marriage rates with the rest of the population as they grow older, which means they get married later in life than their non-disabled peers.

Thirdly, a *larger proportion of disabled women than men get married*. This is true for all age groups and is in line with the pattern for the general population in rural Rajasthan. The NSSO (2003: 17) too found that a greater proportion of disabled women than men get married: while 62 per cent of disabled women had ever been married in rural India, only 53 per cent of disabled men had done so.

However, the NSSO (2003) also reveals that a large proportion of disabled women's marriages are not there to last and that the *rate of widowhood, separation and divorce is much higher* among disabled women than men. About 30 to 31 per cent of disabled women in India were found to be widowed, divorced or separated, which means that every third marriage of disabled women breaks. This is compared to only 7 to 8 per cent of males. The ActionAid survey in Rajasthan too found a much larger proportion of disabled women than men separated, with the proportion of broken marriages among disabled women being three times as high as that of disabled men.

Marriage rates also vary by *type of disability*. The ActionAid survey in Rajasthan found that persons with mental illness or mental retardation are least likely to marry. The NSSO (2003: 16) even suggests that men and women with mental retardation "seem to lead an unmarried life". According to the NSSO, the second most disadvantaged group when it comes to marriage are persons with hearing disabilities. This was not confirmed in this survey here, which found that other than mental retardation and mental illness the hierarchy of marriage rates among different types of disability is less clear-cut and varies across gender.

Marriage: Discussion

The survey data on marriage rates among disabled women presented above goes against previous studies suggesting that the majority of disabled women remain single. The 1996 report on the National Conference of Disabled Women asserts that 80 per cent of disabled women in India remain unmarried. Similarly, a study conducted by the Women's Committee of the Asian Blind Union in 14 states of India in 2000 found that 73 per cent of blind women were not married.[5] A study of 50 disabled women between 18 and 50 years in Kolkata found that 74 per cent of them were unmarried (Sengupta and Ghosh 2003). It is important to note that unlike some of these studies, the ActionAid survey sample was made up not of the urban middle and upper class but of rural women with disabilities with a sample bias towards the poorer sections of village society. This may be the cause of the difference in the study findings.

One possible explanation of the high incidence of marriage among disabled women recorded by the ActionAid survey in rural Rajasthan is that it may be *socially unacceptable* in traditional village society *not to get a daughter married*, as a result of which parents of disabled girls go to any length to secure a match. Naturally, individuals with disability are affected by what the social expectations of adulthood (Groce 2000). According to Sengupta and Ghosh (2003: 5), "the marital status of a girl most often acts as a determining factor of her position in society and family. A girl's life is perceived as ruined or incomplete in Indian society if she remains a spinster all her life". This is because the roles accorded to women in the traditional pockets of Indian society are those of wife and mother with no identity independent of these. Ghai (2002), for example, argues that motherhood is a purpose and identity valorised by Indian culture beyond anything else and is the redemption of a woman's role and status. Accordingly, the denial of marriage and motherhood results in social invisibility, the cancellation of femininity and "rolelessness" (ibid.).

As a result of these strong social compulsions to marry, parents are under pressure to arrange a marriage and "settle" their daughter *at any cost*. "Societal perception of marriage as the final responsibility toward their daughters leads some families to resort to any means, fair or foul, to find them husbands" (Hema 1996). Baquer and Sharma (1997: 193) argue that because a disabled woman gets disqualified on account of her disability in an arranged marriage scenario, parents of a disabled girl are forced to make "a number of compromises" in the selection process. These compromises include marrying their daughter to older men, widowers or as a second wife, as well as offering "exorbitant" amounts of dowry. The Andhra Pradesh and Rajasthan surveys confirmed this. The case studies from the Andhra Pradesh survey suggest that the only people willing to marry a disabled person tend to be widowed, suffer from chronic diseases, live in acute poverty or are looking for a second wife. In Rajasthan, the survey found cases of disabled women being married as second wives, even though bigamy is illegal under Hindu Personal Law. As many as 7 per cent of married women with mental illness and 25 per cent of married women with multiple disability were married to someone as second wives. The survey findings in Andhra Pradesh confirmed that finding a non-disabled match for a disabled daughter in the arranged marriage market typically comes at a high price, as dowry demands are increased to "compensate" for the disability of the bride-to-be. A poor fisher-woman from Visakhapatnam district in Andhra Pradesh, for example, reported dowry demands amounting to Rs 20,000 and two tulas (10 grams) of gold for her disabled daughter.

Neither the Rajasthan nor the Andhra Pradesh survey found *parents of disabled boys* making any such compromises in order to marry off their sons at all cost. Recall from Table 5.1 above that only 44 per cent of the disabled men surveyed were married. One reason could be that social compulsions to get married are much less severe for disabled men than women, with less stigma being attached to an unmarried man who continues to live with his parents. As a result of this parents of disabled boys do not need to bend over backwards and accept even unsuitable matches. At the same time it is also possible that there is a lack of demand in the arranged marriage market for disabled men who are unable to earn a livelihood. Disabled participants in various PRAs said that parents of girls are generally reluctant to accept a disabled son-in-law as they feel that they would be unable to provide financial security for their daughters. Future research exploring the dynamics behind the decision to marry or not to marry would help shed light on the relative importance of these factors.

The analysis above suggested that even though a large number of disabled women get married in rural Rajasthan, many compromises are being made in the process. Being married off at all cost makes disabled women more *vulnerable to desertion* and abuse in marriage. "Even if disabled women do get married, the lasting value of marriage always remains precarious" (Bhambani 2003: 85). This is substantiated by the case studies collected in the Andhra Pradesh survey, which came across many incidents in which the non-disabled partner walked out even after marriage. In some cases the person had not been disabled at the time of marriage, and was deserted when becoming disabled. In other

> Rahmad Bano is now a little over 40 years old. She was a child of twelve years when she got married in Ratlam in Nagaur district of Rajasthan. Just one year after the wedding she fell from the roof of her house and fractured her backbone. Her in-laws kept her for a month without seeking treatment. Finding her of no use, they eventually sent her back to her parental home. Her brothers got her operated but did not proceed with further treatment when their wives objected to the high cost. Soon Rahmad started facing abuse and insults at home, and after some time even the neighbours began to haunt her. When a new marriage proposal came years later, the family was united in pressuring Rahmad to accept. And so she got married to Barkat Ali, who read the *namaaz* and begged for a living. When he was struck by paralysis, Rahmad began to beg herself to sustain the two of them. One year into the marriage, Rahmad gave birth to a child who died of pneumonia in its infancy. During the delivery of the child, her sister-in-law got a vasectomy performed on Rahmad. She justified this by pointing out that two people who depend on the alms of others could not possibly bring up a child. Rahmad says that her relatives shun her because she is poor and disabled.

cases, the disability had been hidden by the family before marriage and the non-disabled partner walked out of the marriage upon discovering the disability. But, in the majority of such case studies, the disabled person was deserted even though the non-disabled partner knew the full extent of the disability at the time of marriage. Recall that the NSSO data cited above also showed a high incidence of desertion, in that every third marriage of a disabled woman in rural India breaks up, with rates of separation or divorce being highest for women with mental illness.

Apart from desertion, disabled women are also vulnerable to *verbal, physical and sexual abuse* in marriage. One needs to note here that the extent of abuse is generally very difficult to quantify, especially in India, where reporting abuse may bring shame to a girl and her family (cf. Johnson and Sujatha 2003: 4). However, thanks to its participatory methodology, the Andhra Pradesh survey nevertheless managed to record many cases of abuse of disabled women. Often these case studies were attained only after surveyors stayed in the house of a disabled woman for several days, thus gaining her trust and being around when she was alone in the house and ready to confide. Female surveyors reported that being disabled women themselves helped them in convincing other disabled village women that they could be trusted and in encouraging them to speak out about their experiences of abuse. Narayanamma's and Venkatsawareamma's cases below represent what many of the disabled women surveyed had to say.

Narayanamma, a disabled woman from Karnool district in Andhra Pradesh, frequently experiences physical and psychological abuse from her non-disabled husband. He does not tire of pointing out that no one else would put up with a disabled woman like her. He cheats on her with another woman in the village. Narayanamma told the surveyors, "If I

> When Chunni Devi of Hirawati village in Nagaur district of Rajasthan was married to Asaram at the age of 15, she did not know that within a year both her parents would die. She could not bear the loss and lost her mental balance. Soon her father-in-law sought a second marriage for his son. He assured Chunni's brother that Chunni would still be allowed to live with her husband and his new wife, that he would bear all her expenditure and that she would be the owner of 20 bigha land. Given these assurances Chunni's brother agreed to the second marriage. Two years later her husband kicked Chunni out of the house. Chunni's brother took her to their parental home and got her treated in a mental hospital in Jaipur. Chunni was better for a short period, before depression took control of her life again. When her husband's property was divided a few years later, Chunni was refused any claim to the land. In protest her brother demanded that either she be given the full 20 bigha land as had been promised or her husband take her back into his house. Her husband decided that taking her back would be a lesser evil than give up his entire land and took Chunni back for a few months, before expelling her once more from his house. Today, she lives with her brother, who built her a small mud hut of her own, where she remains closeted for most of the time, coming out only occasionally to drink water or the like. Living in misery, at the age of 36 Chunni still has half a life before her.

try and raise my voice, he beats me up. Yet if I left my husband, the society would not let me live".

Venkatsawareamma, a locomotor disabled woman from Prakasam district in Andhra Pradesh, is married to a widower. Five months into her marriage her husband started beating her. He eventually sent her back to her parents, saying it was not his duty to provide food to a cripple. When writing up her case study, Venkatsawareamma asked the surveyors, "Why are we disabled people destined to be domestic maids in our own houses? Why does society not recognise that we too are human beings, and free us from this servitude?"

While the above discussion showed that even marriage is by no means a safeguard against desertion and abuse, those disabled people in rural areas who are not able to marry face an even higher risk of destitution and neglect once their parents, typically the primary caretakers, pass away. This is because care and protection responsibilities in India lie with the family and not with the state. The worries of Suramma from Baguvalasa village in Vizainagaram district of Andhra Pradesh reflect this. She says she has tried in vain to find someone who is willing to marry her mentally retarded daughter and has now resigned herself to the fact that it is impossible for her daughter to get married. What pains her most is not the humiliation of being rejected over and over again, but the fact that she has been unable to find someone beside herself to care for her daughter. "What will happen to my daughter after I am gone?" Suramma asks. This is a very real concern. Asiramma, a thirty-year-old unmarried locomotor disabled woman from Vizianagaram district of Andhra Pradesh has been destitute ever since her parents died and is now staying with a Dalit family who took pity on her.

Both in Rajasthan and in Andhra Pradesh the government has sought to facilitate and support marriages of people with disabilities by granting them financial marriage incentives. The state thus addresses one of the barriers to marriage faced by disabled people, namely increased dowry demands on account of their disability. The Social Welfare Department of the Government of Andhra Pradesh issued an order on 25 July 1985 to award Rs 3,000 to either spouse for marriages between "disabled and normal persons".[6] Similarly, the Government of Rajasthan used to provide a one-time grant of Rs 5,000 to couples with one disabled partner, which has been increased to Rs 20,000 in 2003.[7] However, the Andhra Pradesh survey found that 83 per cent of those surveyed were not aware of the marriage incentive scheme and only 7.4 per cent had made use of it.

Consequences of Social Exclusion

We have seen above that it is not the impairment in itself, but negative social attitudes towards the impairment that create the sense of being disabled. It is the social stigma attached to disability which is hardest to bear for disabled people. The Andhra Pradesh survey found some cases in which the social pressure was such that disabled people attempted to escape it by committing suicide. All of the cases of *attempted suicide* found in the survey were motivated by some form of social discrimination and none by the disability itself.

Ramadevi, a 13-year-old girl from Anantapur district in Andhra Pradesh, who has polio and low vision, is one such case. She has faced humiliation time and again from her parents and siblings. Her sister often refuses to take her to school. Her brother took the wheels off her tricycle and fixed them to his own bike instead. Her father justified this by pointing out that a cycle was much more important to her brother than for her, knowing full well that without a tricycle Ramadevi can only move by crawling. She says she is miserable because she is never invited to play with others in school and her parents never take her along to any social functions. One day she overheard the neighbours saying "the pains and difficulties of her parents on account of her will not stop until either she or her parents die". This was just too much to take on top of everything else and Ramadevi tried to hang herself. Ironically, she was rescued by her neighbours. Venkatsawareamma too tried to commit suicide, but was rescued by her brother. She used to face regular abuse by her husband as described above, and faced humiliation by the community after he had eventually sent her back to her parental home. Every time she appeared on the village road people ridiculed her disability and the fact that she had been unable "to keep her husband happy". It was not her locomotor disability but this constant degradation that caused her to attempt suicide. Social ostracism is not only driving disabled people themselves into such despair that they want to end their lives. The survey also found that a young mother of two cerebral palsy boys in Nalgonda district wanted to commit suicide, and that the wife of a speech and hearing impaired person in the same district too had attempted suicide when humiliation from villagers simply became too much for her.

Social ostracism leads to *imprisonment* of disabled people, and sometimes also of their families, *in their own homes*. Sreeramulu and his wife from Warrangal district in Andhra Pradesh have one orthopaedically impaired and two blind children. They say their neighbours have made so many snide comments about what must be wrong with the parents to have so many disabled children that they leave the house as little as possible to avoid being ridiculed. The chapter on education had shown that the same behaviour prevails amongst disabled school children, some of whom stayed at home and quit school because they could no longer take the jeers and ridicule of their peers. The *karma* view of disability discussed above, where a disabled child is seen as evidence of sin, also results in disability being hidden from the public behind the four walls of the home. The consequences of such imprisonment are loneliness and a deep sense of isolation. In 25 per cent of villages covered in the Rajasthan PRAs disabled people said that they felt isolated and depressed. In 20 per cent of villages disabled people said their situation had led to depression and a loss of confidence.

Self-worth may become damaged beyond repair when one is hidden away from the world. In 44 per cent of villages surveyed in Rajasthan disabled people reported an inferiority complex. When a disabled person is considered "a marginal person" from a physical, social and vocational point of view (Bhatt 1985: 83) it is no wonder that the Andhra Pradesh survey widely encountered low self-esteem among them. Some disabled people are considered "marginal" in the physical sense in that they are totally dependent on their caregivers for even the most basic aspects of daily life such as eating, bathing or attending nature's call. From a vocational point of view, disabled people are considered "marginal" when they are unable to find regular gainful employment. Bhambini (2003) argues that the ability to contribute to the family income enhances the worth of an individual in the eyes of other family members. In this view unemployed disabled people not only constitute an economic liability for the family, but are also considered "less worthy".

Policy Recommendations

Previous chapters showed that social exclusion prevents disabled people from engaging in mainstream society across a number of fields, including education, healthcare and livelihoods. Therefore, to combat social exclusion systematically, policy changes are necessary in all these spheres and many of the policy recommendations made in previous chapters address problems of social exclusion just as much as they address problems say in medical care. Policies to promote livelihoods for example, indirectly also address the various problems of social exclusion resulting from economic dependency, such as the perceived inability of some disabled men in villages to get married or the stigma attached to being disabled and poor. Similarly, policies of inclusive education and teacher sensitisation have the potential to eradicate social prejudice and discrimination of entire generations of school children, as growing up with disabled classmates and being taught to respect them is one of the most effective ways in which to change discriminatory attitudes of non-disabled adults-to-be. Policies to extend medical camps and improve the quality of medical disability prevention services are also policies against the invisibilisation of people with disabilities, in so far as corrective surgery on a polio patient would enable a child to go to school and later to work instead of being hidden away in the home out of shame and for lack of mobility.

However, in addition to the policies recommended in previous chapters, there are some measures that can be undertaken to specifically address the *negative attitudes and behaviour* towards people with disabilities in the family, in marriage and in the wider community as described in this chapter.

One such measure is the formation of Self-Help Groups (SHGs) among disabled people, bringing together all disabled people in a village. The power of collectivisation can overcome the paralysis of the individual in dealing with adverse power relationships. During my interaction with disability-SHGs in Andhra Pradesh group members told me that whenever one member of the group was being discriminated against by anyone in the village the perpetrator invariably has the entire group to answer to, be it an employer, teacher, neighbour or family member. Consequently, most members of the group had experienced a reduction in ridicule and humiliation by non-disabled villagers following group formation. Apart from a reactive mechanism of collectively hitting back, some groups had also adopted pro-active initiatives to fight discrimination, such as holding a public meeting in the village explaining the hurtful consequences of prejudiced behaviour by employers, schoolteachers and neighbours. In such meetings they also described to the rest of the village how each of them had acquired the disability and thus tried to dispel notions of disability as bad omens or evidence of sin in a former life. One group had enforced the delivery of state services granted to people with disabilities[8] like aids and appliances or disability certificates by staging a demonstration in front of the disability commissioner's office at district headquarters. The group members proudly told me how quickly the otherwise inconsiderate official had acted on their demands because he was embarrassed, in their words, "to have a bunch of cripples shouting in front of his office".

In order to realise the enormous potential of disability-SHGs to address social exclusion, a couple of procedural precautions need to be kept in mind. Firstly, disability-SHGs should be founded for the purpose of *non-material self-help* with the aim of working collectively for the implementation of the rights of disabled people. They should not be formed as savings and credit SHGs, as has been the case with the disability-SHGs created under the Velugu programme in Andhra Pradesh. Savings and credit SHGs tend to exclude the poorest of the poor (cf. Klasing 2003) and thus are unable to help those among the disabled most vulnerable to discrimination and humiliation. Furthermore, SHGs formed for the purpose of capital mobilisation make the non-material benefits of group participation, e.g., collective defence against discrimination, conditional upon paying what is essentially a high membership fee for an exclusive club.[9] When the tremendous benefits of collectivisation in terms of social exclusion can come for free, there is no reason why disabled people, who are amongst the poorest villagers as demonstrated in the livelihoods chapter, should have to purchase these non-material benefits at the price of forced savings that are never returned. In the case of disability groups, even the argument that savings activities are necessary as a binding factor if the group is to continue to exist is not valid: the realisation of disabled villagers who used to be hidden away in their homes that they are not alone but that many of their problems are shared, as well as the experience that many problems that seemed hitherto insurmountable can actually be solved when addressed collectively is usually enough to sustain participation in the group. So, for the purpose of tackling social exclusion, disability-SHGs are best formed as non-material self-help groups.

It could be argued at this point that quite apart from concerns surrounding social exclusion, savings and credit groups should still be started among the rural disabled in order to improve their access to formal credit. While lack of access to credit for disabled village entrepreneurs is a real problem as discussed in the livelihoods chapter, lending to disability-SHGs is not the solution. When 75 per cent of disabled people in rural Rajasthan reported in the survey that they depend on their family for survival, the majority of disabled villagers are clearly not in a position to contribute savings to a revolving fund. Rather than lending to groups of disabled people, the state needs to provide appropriate credit schemes to disabled individuals. So in the context of disability the enormous potential of SHGs lies not in savings mobilisation, but in combating discrimination in the ways discussed above.

The second precaution that needs to be taken in order to realise the full potential of SHGs in combating social exclusion is that these groups and their federations must be *led by disabled people themselves* and not by the facilitating NGOs. NGOs certainly have a major role to play in taking the lead in the formation of SHGs and encouraging disabled people to participate, as the history of hostile reactions from society experienced by disabled villagers ranging from ridicule in school and the workplace to exclusion from social events needs to be overcome. But, the role of NGOs should not extend beyond that of initiator and facilitator. None of the benefits of SHG formation listed above, like pressuring local government to implement the rights of disabled people or confronting discrimination collectively, can be credibly achieved by lobbying on behalf of the disabled.

The fact that 50 million disabled people in India still live an invisible and silent existence in the early 21st century, unheard and unseen by the rest of the country despite their number, is due to the silence of disabled people themselves and this can only be changed by self-advocacy. It is because the NGOs working in the disability sector have by and large adopted a patronising charity approach that there has been little change in policies and that disabled people are still not a voice to be reckoned with in rural India. Therefore, if SHGs are to have any effect in addressing social exclusion they need to be run by disabled people themselves and must not be patronised by and remain dependent on the NGOs which started them. Recall that the NCPEDP (1998) study discussed in the livelihood chapter revealed that NGOs working on disability are highly reluctant to recruit disabled people into leadership positions. This indicates that self-advocacy is still a distant dream and necessitates a paradigm shift in the approach of many disability NGOs from a "we deliver services for you and speak on your behalf" to "we enable you to demand your rights yourself".

The emergence of strong SHGs in villages across the country could provide the basis of a genuine *disability movement* that adequately represents the real concerns of the majority of disabled people. The present disability movement in India can hardly be called representative since it "advances a few select agendas, mostly those that address the concerns of middle-class men ... agendas visible and significant only for the very privileged of the disabled" (Ghai 2002: 52). Even though 80 per cent of the disabled live in rural areas, the movement is led by a few individuals based in India's metropolises. It is the needs, aspirations and experiences of the other 80 per cent which need to be voiced and politicised if their present state of voicelessness and invisibility is ever to be overcome. And this in turn can only be achieved by disabled people's organisations that deserve the name. Therefore self-led SHGs at the grassroots are necessary building blocks for the emergence of a genuinely representative disability movement. Once strong SHGs have emerged, they need to be linked as SHG federations that can build alliances with other marginalised groups. Only such a bottom-up approach can produce a disability movement that is both more credible and more effective than the present one, because it would be able to mobilise mass support all over the country. In such a scenario politicians, policy makers, development practitioners and the general public could not afford to continue to ignore the needs and demands of disabled people. It would be a different India and there is a long way to go yet.

Another way to address negative behaviour towards people with disabilities and in particular verbal abuse would be to amend the Persons with Disabilities (PWD) Act to include a mention of verbal abuse, but not make it punishable. On a visit to a disability SHG in Uttar Pradesh the present author was told that sneering and ridicule of disabled people in that village had stopped following an official visit by the state's Disability Commissioner, who had declared that calling disabled villagers cripple or other derogatory names was punishable by law. It seems that the mere threat of law is very effective, even though no such law exists at the moment. Even the PWD Act does not address verbal abuse in its present form. An amendment to the Act incorporating a mention thereof would provide the necessary basis for a change in discriminatory behaviour, as it would signal that such behaviour is unacceptable to the state and therefore slowly make the habit unacceptable in general. However, while it is important that verbal abuse finds a mention in the law, it should not be made a punishable offence. Dr Amita Dhanda, chairperson of the PWD Act Amendment Committee, argues that the value of compassion "cannot be established by elbowing".[10] In the realm of attitudes, the legal option is the last resort, and a change in attitude cannot be brought about by coercion.

The problem of limited *participation* of disabled villagers in political and social functions as illustrated by the data presented in the beginning of this chapter is perhaps the most difficult to resolve with any one policy recommendation. As for *political participation*, disabled villagers in as many as 30 PRAs in Andhra Pradesh expressed the desire that disabled people be reserved one seat on each of the village committees formed by the gram sabhas, such as education, hospital, water or endowment committee. They argued that without reservations they would never be granted a voice in village affairs. While reservations may be a necessary step towards political participation, it is not a sufficient one. If disabled people are to be taken seriously in these roles by the rest of the committee and the wider village community they need to become generally visible and active in the village quite apart from the position on the committee. One way to do this is as a member of an SHG. Another is for disability NGOs to involve disabled people in their work. Hema (1996) argues that "this enhanced role, when taken on by the disabled woman, has made her family and her community look at her anew". Unless disabled people are given the opportunity to gain experience in speaking out and acting in public life they will not be able to make active use of reserved committee positions.

As for lack of *participation in private social life*, such as being invited to weddings or having non-disabled friends, this is a tremendous challenge, as it involves changing people's prejudices, anxieties and negative attitudes towards disabled people. One cannot force anybody to invite disabled neighbours to their weddings and other social functions but one can create a public culture with the various policies discussed above where blatant exclusion and humiliation becomes unacceptable. Similarly, one can raise a generation of able-bodied children in inclusive schools for whom it is normal to have disabled friends and classmates and who will consequently not discriminate against disabled persons even as adults. It will take time, but it is worth fighting for given what is at stake.

The root of the situation that disabled people in rural India find themselves in today lies in the social exclusion described in this chapter. The notion of disability being an individual problem and evidence of sin and shame, along with social discrimination results in disabled people being hidden behind the four walls of their home. Being hidden in turn causes isolation, loneliness and silence on the part of the disabled and makes disability as a phenomenon invisible. Invisibilisation in turn causes voicelessness of disabled people despite their significant number. And voicelessness explains the lack of attention from the state and society to disability. It explains why the difficulties facing disabled people at all stages in their life continue to receive only scant attention and why nothing is done to ameliorate their situation. Only breaking this vicious cycle of social prejudice, being hidden away, remaining silent and therefore dispensable to the rest of the world can change the situation of the disabled for the better.

For most of her life Parmina has had to answer to names like Langadi and Lulli, crippled in the legs and arms. The boys of her village shout these names after her and when villagers spot her on the street they say, "look, the cripple is coming". One of her brothers refuses to eat the food she touches, as he alleges it becomes contaminated by her hands which she drags on the ground for stability when walking. While she was still going to school, her classmates used to haunt her and topple her tricycle. Today Parmina's neighbour says, "a girl like her is unfit for marriage". These are moments when even Parmina, who usually has a big smile and brightness in her eyes, has thought of poisoning herself. In those moments she turns to Aasma, her only friend, and shares her grief. And Aasma is also the one who carries Parmina on her back each morning to defecate in the field.

Parmina is twenty and lives in Guraksar village in Hathin block in Faridabad district of Haryana. Her father Ibrahim works as a daily wage labourer and her mother Akhtar also works as an agricultural labourer during the crop season. She has two brothers and lives with her family in a small one-room clay house with a roof made of hay.

When Parmina was two she had a fever. Her parents consulted a doctor, who gave her an injection. Instead of curing the fever, Parmina got polio from the shot. Her parents took her to local doctors, to a nearby mission hospital and even to the B.K. Hospital in Faridabad, but to no avail. Parmina's parents were distraught when told at the mission hospital that it was already too late for cure and that there was "really no use in spending any money on this now". Today both of

Contd. on next page...

Parmina's legs are 100 per cent disabled, as certified by the Chief Secretary of the Haryana Government.

There used to be a time when Parmina attended the primary school in her village. At first her elder brother used to carry her to school every day. Then, when she was in class three, she got a tricycle from the Red Cross and thereafter proudly went to school on her own. But her classmates, who used to call her names and make fun of her, soon started toppling her tricycle time and time again. This made life hell for Parmina, who was reduced to shouting at the other children in helpless frustration. The teacher made things worse by blaming Parmina for any mischief done by the boys in her class. Just when Parmina started to feel that she would no longer be able to take the humiliation and injustice of the teacher's constant accusations, the children's vandalism of her tricycle reached its goal: the tricycle broke and Parmina never went to school again. Today, Parmina says she would still like to study and she would love to learn English, but at twenty years is too old to attend school. "If I could have studied, my life would have been different", she laments.

It is hard to say what the future will hold. At the moment, Parmina does almost all her family's household chores from cooking to cleaning. But she would like to work part-time outside the house too because she enjoys getting out of the house and becomes depressed all alone at home. And she thinks that working and earning money would prove her worth to the many insensitive people around her who, she says, see nothing in her except her disability.

Contd. on next page...

Then there is the question of marriage. Like her neighbour, Parmina's parents believe that no one would marry a girl who practically crawls and whose clothes are consequently dirty and torn. If at all anyone were ever to consider their daughter for marriage, there would surely be an exorbitant demand for dowry, "including a motor bike". For Parmina's family that is simply not affordable. They have heard that the government provides some cash incentives for marrying a person with disability but they don't know about the specifics and are unaware of the implementation of the scheme. They are also worried how their daughter might be treated by her in-laws on account of her disability. "It is best she continues to live with us here" concludes her mother.

Notes

1. A *gram sabha* is a village level body comprised of all people of voting age in the village.
2. A *panchayat* is a village level body of representatives elected by the gram sabha.
3. This was calculated from the data on rural Rajasthan in the 1991 Census of India, Table C-1, Social and Cultural Tables.
4. The term "married" in this section and in both tables is understood as "ever married" and includes those divorced, separated or widowed.
5. The studies by the National Conference of Disabled Women and Asian Blind Union are cited in Bhambani (under publication): "Marriage and Disabled Women in India", entry for an international encyclopedia on disability to be published by Sage.

6. GOMs No. 165, Social Welfare Department, Government of Andhra Pradesh, dated 25 July 1985.
7. p. 5, Rajasthan Social Welfare Department (2002), "Welfare Activities for Persons with Disabilities", Jaipur: Government of Rajasthan.
8. See Annex III.
9. Assuming, as most SHGs I visited in Andhra Pradesh seemed to do, that the group will never be dissolved and that the individual contributions to the revolving fund will therefore never be paid back.
10. In a private communication on 15 June 2004.

REFERENCES

Alkazi, R.M. (1992). Disability. In A. Mukhopadhyay (Ed.), *State of India's Health*. New Delhi: Voluntary Health Association of India.

Alur, M. and Rioux, M. (2004). *Included! An Exploration of Six Early Education Pilot Projects for Children with Disabilities in India*. Bombay: The Spastics Society of India and UNICEF.

Alur, M. (2003). *Invisible Children: A Study of Policy Exclusion*. Bombay: Viva Books.

— (2001). 'Some Cultural and Moral Implications of Inclusive Education in India: A Personal View', *Journal of Moral Education*, 30(3), 287-292.

Arora, R. (2003). 'Poverty and Disability', *Friday Meeting Transactions of Asia Pacific Disability Rehabilitation Journal*, 5 (1), 9-13.

— (2001). 'Demand Augmentation in the Employment Market for Persons with Disabilities', *Asia Pacific Disability Rehabilitation Journal*, 12 (2).

Baquer, A. and Sharma, A. (1997). *Disability: Challenges vs Responses*. New Delhi: Concerned Action Now (CAN).

Barnes, C. and Mercer, G. (2003). *Disability*. Cambridge: Polity.

Barnes, C., Mercer, G. and Shakespeare, T. (1999). *Exploring Disability: A Sociological Introduction*. Cambridge: Polity.

Bhatt, U. (1985). *The Physically Handicapped in India: A Growing National Problem*. Bombay: Popular Book Depot.

Bhambani, M. (2003). Societal Responses to Women with Disability in India. In A. Hans and A. Patri (Eds.), *Women, Disability and Identity*. New Delhi: Sage Publication.

Commonwealth Education Fund India (2003). *Responding to Children with Special Needs: A Review of the Manual for Planning Implementation of Inclusive Education in Sarva Shiksha Abhiyan"*. New Delhi, Unpublished Report.

Coleridge, P. (2000). Disability and Culture. In M. Thomas and M.J. Thomas (Eds.), *Selected Reading Based Rehabilitation Series*. Bangalore: Asia Pacific Rehabilitation Journal Group.

— (1993). *Disability, Liberation and Development*. Oxford: Oxfam.

Datrange, S.A. (2002). 'Employment Creation in Developing Countries'. *ActionAid Disability News*, 12, 36-38.

Deenadayalan, S. (1990). 'Rehabilitation and Disabled People in the Private Sector: Experiences of Titan Watches Ltd'. *ActionAid Disability News*, 1(1), 5-6.

De Haan, A. (2001). *Social Exclusion: Enriching the Understanding of Deprivation*. Brighton: University of Sussex. Available at http://www.sussex.ac.uk/Units/SPT/journal/archive/pdf/issue2-2.pdf

DFID (2000). *Disability, Poverty and Development*. London: Department for International Development.

Disability DK (2002). *Country Strategy India*. Hvidovre: Disability DK. Available at http://www.disiblity.dk/images/docpics/1063886916_India_strategy_samlet version.doc.

Elwan, A. (1999). *Poverty and Disability: A Review of the Literature*. Background Paper for the World Development Report 2000/2001. Washington D.C.: The World Bank.

Erb, S. and Harriss-White, B. (2002). *Outcast from Social Welfare: Adult Disability, Incapacity and Development in Rural South India*. Bangalore: Books for Change.

Ghai, A. (2003). *(Dis)embodied Form: Issues of Disabled Women*. New Delhi: Shakti Books.

— (2002). 'Disabled Women: An Excluded Agenda of Indian Feminism', *Hypatia*, 17(3) 49-66.

Gopalan, S. and Shiva, M. (2000). *National Profile on Women, Health and Development*. New Delhi: Voluntary Health Association of India and World Health Organization.

Groce, N.E. (2000). 'Framing Disability Issues in Local Concepts and Beliefs', *Asia Pacific Disability Rehabilitation Journal*, 10(1), available online at http://www.dinf.ne.jp/doc/english/asia/resource/apdrj/z13j00300/z13j00303.html

Harriss-White, B. (1999). On to a Loser: Disability in India. In B. Harriss-White and S. Subramiam (Eds.), *Illfare in India: Essays on India's Social Sector in Honour of S. Guhan*. New Delhi: Sage.

— (1996). The Political Economy of Disability and Development with Special reference to India, UNIRSD Discussion Paper 73, Geneva: United Nations Institute for Social Development.

Helander, E. (1993). *Prejudice and Dignity: An Introduction to Community Based Rehabilitation*. New York: United Nations Development Programme.

Hema, N.S. (1996). Hopes and Dreams. In D. Driedger, I. Feika and E. Giron Batres (Eds.), *Across Borders: Women with Disabilities Working Together*. Charlottetown: Gynergy Books.

Human Rights Watch (1999). *Broken People: Caste Violence Against India's Untouchables*. New York: Human Rights Watch.

ILO (1996). *Social Exclusion and Anti-poverty Strategy*. Geneva: ILO, available at http://www.ilo.org/public/english/bureau/inst/papers/synth/socex/

Independent Commission on Health (1997). *Report of the Independent Commission on Health in India*. New Delhi: VHAI Press.

Jha, M. M. (2002). *School without Walls: Inclusive Education for All*. Oxford: Heinemann.

Johnson, K. and Sujatha, V. (2003). *Disabled Women: Experience of Abuse, Neglect and Violence*. Bangalore: SABALA and Association of People with Disability.

Karna, G.N. (2000). 'Disability Rights Movement: Conceptual Framework and Its Implications for India', *Disabilities and Impairments,* 14 (1), 15-22.

— (2001). *Disability Studies in India: Retrospects and Prospects*. New Delhi: Gyan Publishing House.

Klasing, I. (2003). *Does Group Lending to SHGs in India Improve Credit Access for the Rural Poor and Reduce Poverty?* Unpublished MA Dissertation. London: School of Oriental and African Studies, University of London.

Kohli, A.S. (1997). *Social Services to Disabled*. New Delhi: Anmol Publications.

Krishna, V.V., Dutt, B.S.V. and Rao, K.H. (2001). *Disabled Persons*. New Delhi: Discovery Publishing.

Krishnaswamy, S. (1987). 'The Demography of the Disabled and the Handicapped in India', *Indian Journal of Social Work,* XVIII (1), 83-94.

Lal, R. (2003). 'Background and Perspective on Disability', *Info Change News & Features*. September Edition, available at http://www.infochangeindia.org/DisabilitiesIbp.jsp#05

Lang, R. (2002). The Role of NGOs in the Process of Empowerment and Social Transformation of People With Disabilities. In M. Thomas and M.J. Thomas (Eds.), *Selected Reading Based Rehabilitation Series*. Bangalore: Asia Pacific Rehabilitation Journal Group.

Mohit, A. (2000). 'Disability in India: Family Responsibility or Social Issue? Sign of a Gradual Paradigm Shift', *Disability World News*.August-September Edition, available at http://www.disabilityworld.org/Aug-Sept2000/International/india.html

Murthy, S. (2003), "Access'Ability?", *Disability India Journal,* September Edition, available at. www.disabilityindiajournal.com

Mukhopadhyay, A. (1992). *State of India's Health*. New Delhi: Voluntary Health Association of India.

Mukhopadhyay, S. and Mani, M.N.G. (2002). Education of Children with Special Needs. In R. Govinda (Ed), *India Education Report*. New Delhi: Oxford University Press.

Naidu, A. (2004). 'People with Disability: Including the Excluded', empowerpoor.org Journal, 1(1), 9-10.

Narayan, J. (2003). 'Healthcare is sick', *Humanscape India*, 10 (9), available at www.humanscapeindia.net

— (1994). 'Special Education in India', *ActionAid Disability News*, 5 (1), 65-66.

NCPEDP (2003). 'The Employment Scenario in India with Reference to People with Disability', available at http://www.dpa.org.sg/DPA/publication/dpipub/fall99/p12.htm

— (1998). *Role of NGOs vis-à-vis The Employment Scenario in India with Reference to People with Disabilities*. New Delhi: National Centre for the Promotion of Employment for Disabled People.

— (1999). 'Employment Practices of the Corporate Sector with Reference to People with Disabilities', *Equity*, 2 (1), 3-5.

Neufeldt, A. and Albright, A. (1998). *Disability and Self-Directed Employment: Business Development Models*. Ottawa, Canada: IDRC/Captus Press.

NHFS (2000). *India National Family Health Survey 1998-1999 (NHFS-2)*. Mumbai: International Institute for Population Sciences.

Novemoney, M.A. and Raj, S.J. (2003). 'A Study on the Status, Family and Socio-Economic Conditions of the Persons with Disabilities in Vallioor Panchayat Union', *Friday Meeting Transaction of Asia Pacific Disability Rehabilitation Journal*, 5(1), 14-20.

NSSO (1991). *A Report on Disabled Persons: NSSO 47th Round, July-December 1991*. Report No. 393. National Sample Survey Organisation, Ministry of Statistics and Programme Implementation. New Delhi: Government of India.

— (2003). *Disabled Persons in India: NSSO 58th Round, July-December 2002*. Report No. 485 (58/26/1). National Sample Survey Organisation, Ministry of Statistics and Programme Implementation. New Delhi: Government of India.

PAC (2002). *The State of India's Public Services: Benchmarks for the New Millennium*. Bangalore: Public Affairs Centre.

Pal, D.K. et al (2002). 'Predictor of Parental Adjustment to Children's Epilepsy in Rural India', *Child Care, Health and Development*, 28 (4), 295-300.

Pande, M. (2003). *Stepping Out: Life and Sexuality in Rural India*. New Delhi: Penguin Books India.

Pandey, R.S. and Advani, L. (1995). *Perspective in Disability and Rehabilitation*. New Delhi: Vikas Publishing House.

Park, K. (1998). *Park's Textbook of Preventive and Social Medicine*. Jabalpur: Banarsidas Bhanet Publishers.

Planning Commission (2001). *Report of the Steering Committee on Social Welfare for the Tenth Five Year Plan (2002-2007)*. TFYP Steering Committee Sl. No. 4/2001. New Delhi: Government of India Planning Commission.

Price, P. (2003). 'Education for All: An Elusive Goal for Children with Disabilities in Developing Countries in the Asian and Pacific Region', *Asia Pacific Disability Rehabilitation Journal*, 14(1), 3-9.

Puri, M. (2003). 'The Disabled Child', *Disability India Journal*. April Edition, available at http://disabilityindia.org/dinJour/articl3.html

Ramdas, G. and Mishra, R.R. (1987). 'Rural Attitude Towards the Disabled', *Indian Journal of Disability and Rehabilitation*, Vol. 1, 49-53.

Rao, V. and Mander, H. (1996). *An Agenda for Caring: Interventions for Marginalised Groups*. New Delhi: Voluntary Health Association of India.

RCI (2000). *Status of Disability in India*. New Delhi: Rehabilitation Council of India.

Seeley, J. (2001). 'Recognising Diversity: Disability and Rural Livelihoods Approaches in India', *ODI Natural Resources Perspectives*, No. 72, 1-4.

Singh (1995), 'Disability and Entrepreneur', *Health for the Millions*, 21(6), 51-52.

Sengupta, S. and Ghosh, J. (2003). *Socialization of Women with Disabilities: A View from West Bengal-India*. Kolkata: ActionAid India, Kolkata Regional Office.

Sundararaman, T., Mander, H., Murthy, A. and Shukla, A.(1996). *Reaching Health to the Poor: Source Book on District Health Management*. Mussoorie: Lal Bahadur Shastri National Academy of Administration.

Thomas, M (1991), 'Technical Aids for Disabled People: Where are We?', *ActionAid Disability News*, 2 (1), 1-3.

UN (1996): *Manual for the Development of Statistical Information for Disability Programmes and Policies*. New York: United Nations.

Wadhwa, S. (2002). 'Guidelines for Evaluation of Disabilities and Procedure for Certification in India', *Childhood Disability Update (June-March), 2-11.*

Werner, D. (1994). *Disabled Village Children*. New Delhi: Voluntary Health Association of India.

— (2002). *Andhra Pradesh Rural Poverty Reduction Project and Community Based Disability Intervention – Preliminary Assessment Report,* available at http://www.velugu.org/downloads/study_reports/davidwerner_disa_report.pdf

WHO (1980). *International Classification of Impairments, Disabilities and Handicaps*. Geneva: World Health Organisation.

— (1993). *Promoting the Development of Young Children with Cerebral Palsy: A Guide for Mid-level Rehabilitation Workers*. Geneva: World Health Organisation.

Yeo, R. and Moore, K. (2003). 'Including Disabled People in Poverty Reduction Work: Nothing About Us Without Us', *Action on Disability and Development,* 31(3), 571-590.

Yeo, R. (2001). Chronic Poverty and Disability, *Chronic Poverty Research Centre Working Paper 4,* Manchester: Institute of Development Policy and Management/CPRC.

INDEX